Physical Characteristics of the Soft Coated Wheaten Terrier

(from the American Kennel Club breed standard)

Back: Strong and level.

Body: Compact; relatively short coupled.

Tail: Docked and well set on, carried gaily but never over the back.

Hindquarters: Hind legs well developed with well bent stifles turning neither in nor out; *hocks* well let down and parallel to each other. Feet are round and compact with good depth of pad.

Coat: An abundant single coat covering the entire body, legs and head; coat on the latter falls forward to shade the eyes. Texture soft and silky with a gentle wave. For show purposes, the Wheaten is presented to show a terrier outline, but coat must be of sufficient length to flow when the dog is in motion.

Size: A dog shall be 18 to 19 inches at the withers, the ideal being 18.5. A bitch shall be 17 to 18 inches at the withers, the ideal being 17.5. Dogs should weigh 35-40 pounds; bitches 30-35 pounds.

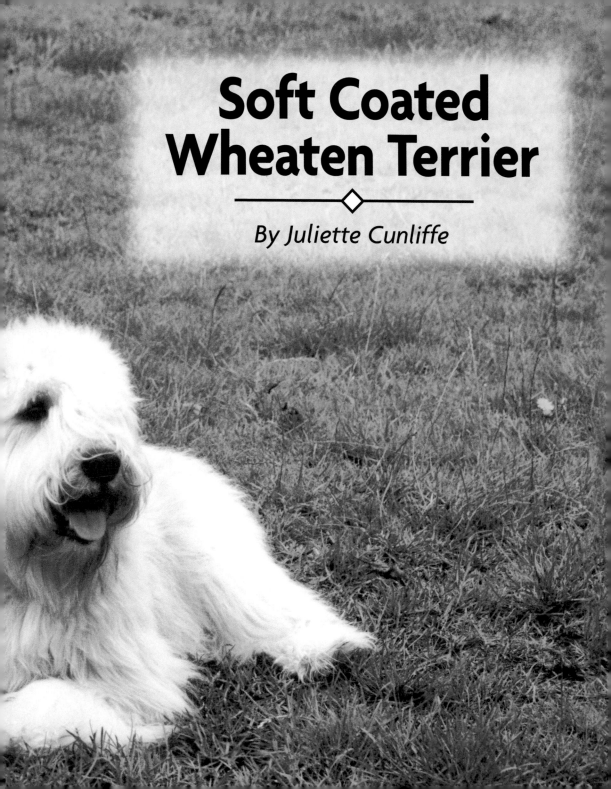

Soft Coated Wheaten Terrier

◇

By Juliette Cunliffe

Contents

Training Your Soft Coated Wheaten Terrier   **87**

Begin with the basics of training the puppy and adult dog. Learn the principles of house-training the Soft Coated Wheaten Terrier, including the use of crates and basic scent instincts. Enter Puppy Kindergarten and introduce the pup to his collar and leash, and progress to the basic commands. Find out about obedience classes and other activities.

Healthcare of Your SCWT   **111**

By Lowell Ackerman DVM, DACVD
Become your dog's healthcare advocate and a well-educated canine keeper. Select a skilled and able veterinarian. Discuss pet insurance, vaccinations and infectious diseases, the neuter/spay decision and a sensible, effective plan for parasite control, including fleas, ticks and worms.

Showing Your Soft Coated Wheaten Terrier   **143**

Step into the center ring and find out about the world of showing pure-bred dogs. Here's how to get started in AKC shows, how they are organized and what's required for your dog to become a champion. Take a leap into the realms of obedience trials, agility trials and more.

KENNEL CLUB BOOKS®
SOFT COATED WHEATEN TERRIER

ISBN: 1-59378-303-5

Copyright © 2004, **2007** • Kennel Club Books® • A Division of BowTie, Inc.
40 Main Street, Freehold, NJ 07728 USA
Cover Design Patented: US 6,435,559 B2 • Printed in South Korea

Photography by Carol Ann Johnson
with additional photographs by

Ashbey Photography, Mary Bloom, Paulette Braun, T.J. Calhoun, Carolina Biological Supply, David Dalton, Fleabusters Rx for Fleas, Isabelle Français, Bill Jonas, Dr. Dennis Kunkel, Tam C. Nguyen, Phototake, Jean Claude Revy and Karen Taylor.

Illustrations by Patricia Peters.

The publisher wishes to thank all of the owners whose dogs are illustrated in this book, including Zara Petit, Marjorie and Dan Shoemaker and Lisa Thompson.

Once the dog of Ireland's poor, the SCWT is now a popular pet and show dog around the world.

HISTORY OF THE

SOFT COATED
WHEATEN TERRIER

The Soft Coated Wheaten Terrier is an Irish breed, and Ireland is a country that abounds in folklore and legend. Unfortunately for us, the history of dogs in Ireland tends to be passed down by word of mouth rather than in writing, making it difficult to be entirely clear as to what happened in the breed's dim and distant past.

Let us begin by taking ourselves back to ancient times, when there were already references to dogs native to Ireland. The Romans are said to have held Irish dogs in high regard, so much so that such dogs were reproduced on coins, on tapestries and on musical instruments. These were, of course, the dogs that hunted with the nobility, but there were other smaller dogs in Ireland too. These were called "cotters" dogs, and included Ireland's early terriers. It is worth noting that Ireland's earliest canine archeological evidence is the bone of a dog believed to be of terrier type.

In 17th-century Ireland, only the gentry were allowed to keep hounds, greyhounds and land-spaniels. The terrier was the "poor man's dog" and was used by farmers as a general-purpose dog, protecting both people and property. Such dogs could herd sheep and work cattle, and were of great use in keeping down vermin. They hunted foxes as well as badgers and otters, both on land and in water, and there are reports of some even having been used with the gun. These were intelligent dogs, big enough to show their authority, yet not so big that they were excessively expensive to keep. At one time it was said that this was "the best dog ever for poaching."

An irresistible Soft Coated Wheaten Terrier puppy, showing great promise as a winner of ribbons and hearts!

THEORY OF ORIGIN

Although it is impossible to know exactly how the Soft Coated Wheaten Terrier came about, there is a theory that the breed evolved from Portuguese Water Dogs that were used as couriers between ships during the time of the Spanish Armada. It is suggested that some of these dogs swam to Ireland after their ships sank, and that survivors bred with the local terriers.

The Kerry Blue Terrier may have derived from Wheatens breeding with large blue shipwrecked dogs that swam to the shores of Ireland.

It is difficult to say when the Soft Coated Wheaten Terrier emerged as a specific breed, but it is thought to be over 200 years old. In the areas around Cork and Wicklow in southern Ireland, and Ballymena in what is now Northern Ireland, there were references to long-legged terriers, wheaten in color and with open coats.

TERRIERS OF IRELAND

It is likely that the three long-legged terriers of Ireland—the Irish, Kerry Blue and Soft Coated

Wheaten—are closely related, as indeed is the Glen of Imaal Terrier, which is much lower to the ground. It is likely that the Soft Coated Wheaten is the oldest of these four breeds, and this is certainly borne out by the fact that the wheaten color crops up from time to time in the Kerry Blue Terrier. This is a recessive trait and can hence lie dormant for generations, thus bearing no reflection on the recent pureness of pedigree of sire and dam. In years gone by, terriers in Ireland were undoubtedly interbred.

An often-told story of the origin of the Kerry Blue is that

following a shipwreck in 1775, a large blue dog swam ashore to Ireland, where it mated with a wheaten-colored terrier, bringing about the Kerry Blue Terrier breed known so well today. Indeed, in the 18th century, the Wheaten is said to have been numerous.

It is generally agreed that the Wheaten is of somewhat mixed ancestry, and it would appear that they were allowed to mate freely with other breeds, although clearly the breed's many qualities gave good reason for enthusiasts to want to maintain its type. Having said that, for a good while there was some confusion with the breed described as the Irish Terrier, as can be seen from show reports from the latter part of the 19th century. Undoubtedly, deliberate

> **WORK OF ART**
> An engraving by F. Bacon, dated 1843, is titled *The Aran Fisherman's Drowned Child*. This clearly shows a Soft Coated Wheaten Terrier in the foreground, mourning the dead child as if the dog were a family member.

The Irish Terrier, as a distinct breed, is represented by this modern show dog, which captures the breed's graceful racy appearance.

breeding experiments took place, and Irish Terrier enthusiasts made every effort to breed dogs that adhered in type to the standard set down by their own breed club.

Because of the lack of written documentation, it is difficult to know where divisions between the various breeds actually lay. However, in the second half of the 19th century, there were some thoroughly absorbing reports from shows in Ireland. In 1873, the *Live Stock Journal* said of the class of Irish Terriers at the Dublin show that the dogs were all of different types and had "no reason to be called Irish, except that they had Ireland as a birthplace!"

The least known of the Irish terriers, the Glen of Imaal Terrier from County Wicklow, a game and spirited long-bodied terrier, colored in blue, wheaten or brindle.

By 1874, the Dublin show offered prizes for Irish Terriers under 9 pounds in weight, while in 1876 there were 34 entries for Irish Terriers above 16 pounds and below 16 pounds. Of particular interest is that, at this show, the judge had been selected because he had been a breeder of "wild Irishmen" for 20 or 30 years, and so had special knowledge. It was believed that his findings would meet with general approval and would settle, once and for all, the question of type. However, contrary to expectations, the results gave rise to "a wailing and gnashing of teeth." Prizes went to long legs, short legs, hard coats, soft coats, thick skulls and long thin skulls, and some prizewinners were mongrels.

The following is part of an amusing poem, published after this particular show and called *"The Wail of the Irish Terrier"*:
"My father came from Limerick,
My mother came from York;
A half-bred Yorkshire blue-and-tan,
They hailed me from Cork;
An Irish terrier I was called,
And sent on bench to show,
But oh! How little they believed
I should cause such a row!"

The above is intended just to give the reader a small taste of the confusion that reigned in Ireland prior to the turn of the 20th century. It is prudent to add that at that time the Irish Terrier was required to have a coat that "Must

> **BREED NAME CONTROVERSY**
> There was certain controversy surrounding the name of the breed in the early days. "Irish Wheaten Terrier" was at first suggested, but breeders of the Irish and Glen of Imaal Terriers were very much opposed to this, as the color "wheaten" was an accepted color for each of these breeds. Indeed, wheaten was then the preferred color for Irish Terriers.

be hard, rough and wiry, in decided contradistinction to softness, shagginess and silkiness, and all parts perfectly free from lock or curl." Clearly it was the Irish Terrier that we know today to which this description was aimed, but it is also clear that today's Soft Coated Wheaten Terrier was at that time among their ranks.

THE TERRIER BREEDS DIVIDE
The first breed standard for the Irish Terrier was drawn up in 1880 but, as we have already seen, dogs with open or soft coats were often benched with them. The colors of these soft-coated dogs could include blue, gray, silver and wheaten. Only from 1914 onward was the Kerry Blue separated as a distinct breed. The Soft Coated Wheaten was the last of Ireland's terriers to be recognized as a distinct breed,

apparently because some influential people had a vested interest in other of the terrier breeds, thereby preventing the Soft Coated Wheaten from making the necessary progress. Mr. Patrick Blake, who was a Kerry Blue fancier, had been highly impressed by a Wheaten Terrier that performed especially well at a field trial in 1932, and he was determined to guide the breed away from obscurity and possible extinction. With his friend Dr. G. J. Pierse, in 1934 Blake founded the Softcoated Wheaten Terrier Club, and several applications for recognition were made to the Irish Kennel Club. Recognition was finally granted in 1937, when the official name "Softcoated Wheaten Terrier" was adopted and the breed was presented at the Irish Kennel Club Show in Dublin, held on St. Patrick's Day. In 1939, the breed was recognized as a National Breed.

The breed is highly trainable and excels in agility trials. This Wheaten is clearing the bar jump at an agility trial.

A WORKING TERRIER

For many years, the Soft Coated Wheaten Terrier was employed for the work of hunting both otters and badgers. This was a difficult job and, when the breed was entered in field trials, it often took prizes more consistently than did other breeds, thereby establishing itself as one of Ireland's top working terriers.

In the breed's early days at Irish shows, to become a full Irish champion, a certificate of gameness was also required. There were two necessary trials, minor and major. In the minor trial, the dog had to go after rabbits, showing an interest in them by following the scent persistently and, if possible, catching one. This test also involved releasing rats into a canal, and the dog was expected to go in after the rats without hesitating. For the second test, the major, a badger was sent into a winding tunnel and the terrier was then released into the tunnel. The dog had to find the badger within one minute and then had six minutes to make contact, but without making a noise. It was better still if the dog pulled the badger out! These trials were mercifully outlawed in the mid-1960s, so that from then on Soft Coated Wheatens could become champions in the show ring without proving their prowess with game.

There were two main reasons for outlawing these trials. In the first instance, they were considered cruel and, as a result, were giving the breeds involved with them a bad name. Secondly, it was rumored that other breeds were being introduced into breeding programs in an endeavor to make the dogs more game, which was damaging breed type. Nonetheless, it is known that secret badger trials took place for many years after they had been officially banned.

The Soft Coated Wheaten was recognized in Britain in 1943, but by 1950 it had still not yet gathered many supporters on the other side of the Irish Sea. However, the breed was doing fairly well in Ireland, with 18 dogs entered at the Irish Terrier Club's show that year.

BATTLE OF THE SCISSORS
Mrs. Maureen Holmes had her first Soft Coated Wheaten Terrier

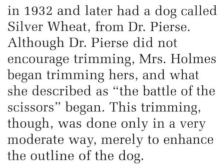

in 1932 and later had a dog called Silver Wheat, from Dr. Pierse. Although Dr. Pierse did not encourage trimming, Mrs. Holmes began trimming hers, and what she described as "the battle of the scissors" began. This trimming, though, was done only in a very moderate way, merely to enhance the outline of the dog.

In 1950, Soft Coated Wheatens were entered at Crufts, but after a few years of success it is said that in England their appearance changed dramatically, almost overnight. The Irish dogs that appeared at Crufts soon looked out of place and were disregarded by judges.

Although in Ireland every endeavor has been made to keep to breed type, this seems not to have been so in all countries. The Irish breed club has tried to educate newcomers to the breed, warning them when the club felt that the breeders were straying from typicality. Over the years, there has been some concern about the fact that Irish breeders sent abroad too many of their own Soft Coated Wheaten Terriers, this at the risk of not retaining sufficient numbers of high-quality stock in the breed's homeland.

THE WORLD CONGRESS OF KENNEL CLUBS IN DUBLIN
An especially important year for the Soft Coated Wheaten Terrier was 1995, for the World Congress

IRISH LAW
It is interesting sometimes to research early laws, for often they have references to our canine friends. In Ireland, during the 18th century, tenant farmers were actually prohibited from owning any dog with a value greater than £5.

TERRA

The word "terrier" actually comes from the Latin word *terra*, which means earth. All such dogs carrying this name were selectively bred to be not only very brave but also tough. It is generally accepted that most terriers originated in the British Isles, where they have been known since the Middle Ages.

of Kennel Clubs was held in Dublin, and the Irish breeds were the main topics for the seminars. By then, the Soft Coated Wheaten had spread to 22 countries throughout the world, but concern was expressed that some of the dogs entered at FCI (Fédération Cynologique Internationale) shows no longer fitted the Irish (FCI) standard and, in consequence, there was a risk of losing true breed type.

It was most unfortunate that Mrs. Maureen Holmes, the longest established breeder of Soft Coated Wheatens, was unable to be present at the Congress because she was hospitalized. However, her own strong views were conveyed by Mr. Tony Killykeen Doyle, Chairman of Ireland's specialist breed club. Before passing on some of Mrs. Holmes's comments, it is important to mention that for over 40 years she was the breed representative to the Irish Kennel Club and also

had carried out several offices within the breed club, including that of President. Through her Holmenocks Kennel, Mrs. Holmes worked hard for the promotion and recognition of the Soft Coated Wheaten Terrier, both in Ireland and abroad, and was author of two books about the breed. Sadly, she passed away in 1996.

Mrs. Holmes wished to bring attention to the fact that "some retired American champions of a different type, style and build" had been used extensively at stud. She considered that because of the American dogs' smart, flashy appearance, they had almost decimated the sturdy Irish type.

Most breed enthusiasts, whether or not they are owners of Soft Coated Wheatens, would surely agree that there are very evident differences in the appearance of the breed from country to

The Wheaten was recognized in Britain in 1943 and is frequently seen taking home ribbons at the shows. This modern dog is winning at Crufts, Britain's premier competition.

country; how they view these differences is for each to decide for himself. However, as conveyed at the Congress, Mrs. Holmes was very open in her personal view that the breed had been brought to what she called "the brink of disaster" by indiscriminate breeding. She believed that dogs were part of a country's heritage and, like other valuable things, should be preserved.

SOFT COATED WHEATEN TERRIERS IN AMERICA

The first SCWTs to arrive in the US were a breeding pair imported by Lydia Vogels of Springfield, Massachusetts in November 1946. Some 17 puppies were produced from this pair. Although Vogels's dogs were shown with some success in the AKC Miscellaneous Classes, there was insufficient interest in the breed for it to receive full championship status by the AKC. The breed was exhibited at the famous Westminster Kennel Club Dog Show in 1947, but it did not take hold until the O'Connors (of Brooklyn, New York) and the Arnolds (of Connecticut) imported some dogs in the 1950s.

It was about ten years after Lydia Vogels's initial import that the O'Connor family brought in a bitch named Holmenocks Gramachree from Maureen Holmes, the most influential breeder in Ireland. It was through

seeing picture of Lydia Vogels's Soft Coats that the O'Connors had fallen in love with the breed. The "shaggy dog" look attracted them.

The O'Connors decided they would like the breed to be granted AKC recognition and so, with the help of Maureen Holmes, they tracked down descendents of the Vogels's dogs and other Irish imports. This led to the formation of the Soft Coated Wheaten Terrier Club of America (SCWTCA), on March 17, 1962, St. Patty's Day! However it was believed that there were fewer than 30 representatives of the breed in the country. Influential dogs from these early days, owned by the O'Connors and Arnolds, include Holmenocks Hallmark, Gads Hill, Liam and Maud.

But things moved ahead steadily and a stud book was commenced in 1965. By 1968 there were 280 Soft Coated Wheatens registered. The club held its first matches in 1970 and 1971, but the breed remained in the Miscellaneous Class, where large numbers of Wheatens flooded the ring in an effort to show the AKC that the breed was ready for the big time! In October 1973 the Soft Coated Wheaten Terrier was allowed to compete in the Terrier Group, thanks to the clever guidance of Dan and Marjorie Shoemaker. In addition to the O'Connors, Arnolds and Shoemakers, Jacqueline Gottlieb,

her daughter Cindy Gottlieb Vogels, Emily Holden, Carol Carlson, Eileen Jackson, Ida Mallory and Gay Sherman Dunlap are among the other breeders whose dedication and hard work led to the SCWT's success in the US during the first ten years of AKC recognition.

Dan Shoemaker served as the Soft Coated Wheaten Terrier Club of America's first president for the first five years. The club drew up its own standard of points, which was adopted by the American Kennel Club. Champion Abby's Postage Dhu O'Waterford, owned by Dan and Marjorie Shoemaker, became the breed's first AKC champion.

From the late 1960s onward, the breed has continued to increase in popularity in the US, so that by the early 1990s it had become the seventh most popular terrier breed in the country. Annual

registrations with the AKC had risen to over 2,000 per year; a great leap forward from the numbers of the 1960s. There are local SCWT breed clubs in ten states plus the District of Columbia.

Canada also has a "soft" spot for the Wheaten. Ruth Cronk of British Columbia imported the first SCWT to Canada in 1969. The first Canadian-born litter was whelped by Appl and Ruth Gunther of Saskatchewan in 1977. The parents were American imports. Full recognition of the SCWT by the Canadian Kennel Club was attained in 1978 thanks to the determination of British Columbia residents Alan Fox and Anne Goodsell. Today the Soft Coated Wheaten Terrier Association of Canada continues to promote and protect the breed and publishes a quarterly newsletter called the *Wheaten Wags*.

A handsome lineup of American-bred SCWTs showing off their well-groomed "terrier outlines."

With a joy for living and steadfast loyalty to his family, the Wheaten is an excellent choice for an active, interactive household.

CHARACTERISTICS OF THE
SOFT COATED WHEATEN TERRIER

WHY THE SOFT COATED WHEATEN TERRIER?

Although its name might be appealing, whether or not any owners have been drawn to the Soft Coated Wheaten Terrier by its name is perhaps debatable, for it has to be admitted that it is rather a mouthful! When writing about the breed, the initials SCWT are frequently used, so I hope readers will not mind my using them here.

This is a breed about which there is a lot to like. The SCWT has stamina, gameness, strength, intelligence and a joy for living, as indeed have other of the terrier breeds. However, the SCWT is somewhat steadier than many other terriers, and is incredibly loyal to its family. Having said that, to be fair, SCWTs are not perfect pets for everyone, as they can be somewhat stubborn and rather headstrong.

PERSONALITY

The SCWT is a natural terrier, and one that has strong sporting instincts. The breed should be spirited and game, but good-

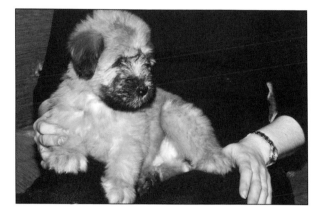

The SCWT pup should possess the affection and humor with which the breed has come to be associated.

tempered with plenty of confidence. This is a delightful companion, affectionate and intelligent, and the breed seems to have a marvelous sense of humor.

This breed manages to combine the alert intelligence of the terrier with the steadiness of a working dog, which is an admirable combination. As puppies, SCWTs are exuberant, and somehow they still have that joy for living in adulthood and retain a medium to high energy level throughout their lives.

SCWTs do like to be close to the people of whom they are most fond, and seem happy to adapt to

The Wheaten is a fine choice for a home with children, provided that the children take an active part in the SCWT's education and rearing.

firm, it should never under any circumstances be harsh. It is important that a Wheaten be taught to respect his owner, but the breed's high spirit should never be broken. Although SCWTs can be trained, they need a firm hand. In general, training requires somewhat more time and dedication from the owner than would be required for many other breeds.

THE SCWT WITH CHILDREN AND OTHER PETS

This is a breed that generally gets along well with children; with children they can be very loving. However, dogs and small children should always be introduced under careful supervision so that accidents never occur. Young children should be taught not to pull at the SCWT's rather appealing long coat! If socialized when young, the SCWT also gets along reasonably with other dogs, but cats can be quite a different matter. Because cats move quickly, the terrier instinct is

life in either the country or the city. Wherever they live, it is important that they be given plenty of time and attention. The SCWT must be taught to accept its standing in the family's pecking order, for the dog often wants to be the leader and can be a little headstrong.

Discipline should be given consistently; while this should be

SPLASH!
Some SCWTs absolutely love water, and swimming can indeed be fun if carefully supervised. One should never assume, though, that all Wheatens like water, for some seem to despise it. It is, however, safe to say that, being an energetic breed, they will love to go for walks.

easily alerted, and "attack" is frequently the next step. As with so many breeds, it may indeed be possible to bring up a dog alongside the family cat, but a strange cat encountered in the yard will usually need to make a very rapid get-away.

As with the other terrier breeds, SCWTs are keen to chase small rodents. If the family's other pet is something like a guinea pig or a hamster, it should be kept out of harm's way!

PHYSICAL CHARACTERISTICS

This is a compact, relatively short-coupled, upstanding terrier

SOFT AT HEART?
The Soft Coated Wheaten Terrier should always be socialized with other dogs while still young. Although not as aggressive as some of the other breeds in the Terrier Group, males can be only too happy to stand up to another dog if challenged!

The SCWT raised with children will grow up to be a protective, devoted companion to them.

that is strong and well built. The SCWT is not exaggerated in any way and is well balanced in both structure and movement. When not moving, the dog should stand four square, with head and tail up. These are features of the breed that help show that this is a happy dog, one that is full of character.

HEAD AND EARS

The moderately long skull of the SCWT is of medium width, but should never be coarse. Indeed the American Kennel Club breed standard gives a clear and detailed description of the foreface and skull, which should be of equal length. The skull is flat and the stop defined, while the nose should always be black and large for the dog's face.

The V-shaped, thin ears are folded at the level of the skull, their forward edge dropping down slightly so that it lies closely along the cheek. The back edge of the ear stands slightly away from the head. The clear, bright, dark reddish brown or brown eyes, with their black eye rims, are medium in size and set under a strong brow.

TAIL

The tail of the SCWT is customarily docked, so that in an adult the length of tail is about 4–5 inches. The tail of the SCWT should be set on high and carried gaily, but this is a terrier breed and the tail should never be carried over the back.

SIZE

The SCWT is a medium-sized breed, with dogs standing approximately 18–19 inches at withers. They weigh 35–40 pounds, while in both height and weight bitches tend to be a little smaller than males.

MOVEMENT

The SCWT moves with long, low strides, and is well coordinated in its movement, which is free, graceful and lively. There is both

DELTA SOCIETY

The human-animal bond propels the work of the Delta Society, striving to improve the lives of people and animals. The Pet Partners Program proves that the lives of people and dogs are inextricably linked. The Pet Partners Program, a national registry, trains and screens volunteers for pet therapy in hospices, nursing homes, schools and rehabilitation centers. Dog-and-handler teams of Pet Partners volunteer in all 50 states, with nearly 7,000 teams making visits annually. About 900,000 patients, residents and students receive assistance each year. If you and your dog are interested in becoming Pet Partners, contact the Delta Society online at www.deltasociety.org.

forehand reach and good drive from behind. When moving, the topline should remain level. Both head and tail are carried high.

COAT

The coat of the SCWT is different from that of any other terrier, for it is soft and silky, loosely waved. The UK standard allows curls, saying that curls should be large, light and loose if present. In all cases, the coat should flow and fall naturally, not standing off from the body. Although the coat is abundant all over the body, it is especially profuse on the head and the legs. It is worth noting that the

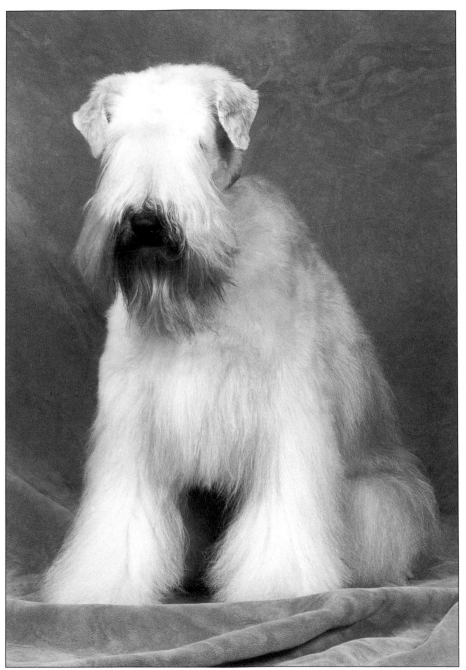

The most contro-versial breed issue involves the SCWT's coat, which is groomed variously around the world. This elegant SCWT is a show-winning dog in the US.

texture of the coat does not stabilize until the dog is around two years of age.

Presentation of the SCWT's coat is a highly controversial issue and differs greatly around the world. In the United States, for show purposes, the SCWT is presented to show a terrier outline, but the coat must be of sufficient length to flow when the dog is in motion. Apart from the difference in bodily outline, the "head coat should be blended to present a rectangular outline." In Britain, The Kennel Club's breed standard includes the words "Over-trimming or stylizing

should be penalized. For show purposes the coat may be tidied to present a neat outline." In Ireland, dogs may be shown trimmed or untrimmed, but dogs that are "fluffed out" are heavily penalized.

This is a matter for constant debate, and the way in which an SCWT's coat is presented will depend upon the country in which your dog is shown. This is a very important consideration for any overseas exhibitors with any aspirations of showing the SCWTs in the US. The Wheatens winning in AKC show rings are far more elegant and artfully

The colors of the SCWT are the varying shades of wheaten. This line-up of British show dogs illustrates the "natural" untrimmed coat style favored in the UK.

DIFFERING TYPES
Most people involved with the Soft Coated Wheaten Terrier will agree that, in effect, there are actually three differing types—Irish, English and American. Indeed, sometimes the dogs differ more greatly from country to country than is apparent from merely reading the countries' breed standards.

sculpted than the rugged blokes winning in the UK.

Because the SCWT does not shed a great deal of hair if groomed correctly, it can be a sensible choice for allergy sufferers. However, before purchasing any dog, allergy sufferers should be absolutely certain that the breed they have chosen is one that is unlikely to cause them any discomfort. You and your family should have exposure to a Wheaten in a contained atmosphere before making a final decision.

COLOR

The AKC breed standard simply calls for "any shade of wheaten." The British standard puts it more poetically, describing the color as a "shade of ripening wheat." Although dark shading on the ears is not untypical, white and red coats are both objectionable. In Ireland, the breed standard requires the coat color simply to be "Any shade from light wheaten to a golden reddish hue." Regardless of word choice, the overall coloring must be clearly wheaten, with no evidence of any other color, except that blue-gray shading is sometimes present on the ears and muzzle.

SCWT puppies are born dark in color, perhaps best described as the color of a brown paper bag, but their color changes as they mature. As for the texture of the coat, the coat color in SCWTs cannot be expected to stabilize until around 24 months of age, the overall darker color and dark markings having cleared by then. This understandably needs to be taken into consideration when selecting a puppy.

TEETH

As is true of other terriers, the teeth are quite large for the size of the dog. The Wheaten's pearly whites can be seen in a typical canine scissors bite or a level bite. Teeth should be set square to the jaws, which should be strong.

HEALTH CONSIDERATIONS

In general, the Soft Coated Wheaten Terrier is a healthy dog, and, if given proper care with correct feeding, this is a breed that should lead a long and active life. However, all breeds encounter health problems of one sort or another, and as time moves on and genetic research progresses,

HEART-HEALTHY
In this modern age of ever-improving cardio-care, no doctor or scientist can dispute the advantages of owning a dog to lower a person's risk of heart disease. Studies have proven that petting a dog, walking a dog and grooming a dog all show positive results toward lowering your blood pressure. The simple routine of exercising your dog—going outside with the dog and walking, jogging or playing catch—is heart-healthy in and of itself. If you are normally less active than your physician thinks you should be, adopting a dog may be a smart option to improve your own quality of life as well as that of another creature.

more and more problems come to light. This can only be for the future benefit of dogs, though to read about any disease can be somewhat alarming, especially for newcomers to dogs.

Nonetheless, to be forewarned is to be forearmed, so the following section of this chapter is not intended to put fear into those who are considering becoming Soft Coated Wheaten Terrier owners. The Soft Coated Wheaten Terrier Club of America recommends health screening for PLE, PLN, RD and Addison's disease. Here's some basic

information about these and other inherited diseases.

PLE AND PLN
The SCWT has an inherited predisposition for diseases that cause protein loss. PLE stands for protein-losing enteropathy, involving loss from the intestine; PLN stands for protein-losing nephropathy, involving loss from the kidneys. Most researchers believe that the two conditions are related, and sometimes PLN and PLE are found in the same dog.

Often there is no sign of illness until middle age, by which time a dog may have been bred from, and presently there are no tests to determine which dogs may become ill later in their lives. Research is currently underway, for the mode of inheritance is not yet proven, and environmental factors may play a part.

PLN is difficult to diagnose. In consequence, the initial signs can be mistaken for liver, glandular or other enteric or kidney diseases. Indeed clinical signs vary, but can include listlessness and depression, decreased appetite, weight loss and vomiting. These can be severe and can lead to death. Tissue biopsies frequently show inflammatory bowel disease, and it has been demonstrated that the disease is associated with food allergies.

PLE is most frequently caused by an inflammatory bowel disease, with a stimulation of the immune system in the bowel wall. Among the common signs of PLE are vomiting, diarrhea and loss of weight.

RENAL DYSPLASIA

Renal dysplasia (RD) has appeared as a problem in the SCWT and, again, research is being carried out on this disease. It involves congenital malformation or abnormal development of the kidneys, and is generally apparent before two years of age.

The first clinical symptom usually observed in affected dogs is an increase in the production of urine, coupled with excessive thirst. When the urine is checked, it is found to be extremely dilute, this being indicative of kidney disease. Later a dog may lose appetite and have muscular weakness, vomiting, diarrhea and foul-smelling breath.

SCWTs bred for the show ring must be flawless inside and out—healthy and handsome.

HEALTHY DOGS

In 1991 an interesting health survey of SCWTs was carried out by an American university. Of those surveyed, 93% of owners reported that their dog's overall health was good. Of the 35% seen by vets for non-routine healthcare, the most common causes were in the following order: diarrhea, skin problems, cancer, teeth and throat problems and musculoskeletal problems.

Although there is no cure, initially the clinical symptoms can often be reduced by feeding a low-protein diet, usually one that has been specially prescribed.

ADDISON'S DISEASE

Addison's disease, also known as hypoadrenocorticism, has been cited in the SCWT. This disease of the adrenal gland cortex is characterized by the insufficient production and secretion of glucocorticoids and mineralocorticoids. Among the symptoms recognized are listlessness, depression, decreased appetite, weight loss, vomiting and other signs that can be attributed to many other medical problems. Screening tests are available, which include biochemical profile, complete blood count and urinalysis. Eye clearances must be certified by an American College of Veterinary Ophthalmologists (ACVO) board ophthalmologist. Records are kept by the Canine Eye Registration Foundation (CERF). All breeders are expected to test their dogs before mating.

PROGRESSIVE RETINAL ATROPHY
Progressive retinal atrophy, usually referred to as PRA, is a complex of inherited eye disorders, not usually discovered until adulthood, in which a dog progressively goes blind. This is often first noticed by night-blindness, but total blindness is unfortunately the inevitable end result. Thankfully, there is no pain.

Breeders have to use their carefully considered knowledge of hereditary factors to avoid, if possible, doubling up on the gene that carries this inherited disease.

HIP DYSPLASIA
Hip dysplasia is a problem involving the malformation of the ball and socket joint at the hip, a developmental condition caused by the interaction of many genes. This results in looseness of the hip joints and, although not always painful, it can cause lameness and can impair typical movement.

Although a dog's environment does not actually cause hip dysplasia, it may have some bearing on how unstable the hip joint eventually becomes. Osteoarthritis can eventually develop as a result of the instability.

Tests for hip dysplasia are available and are sent to the Orthopedic Foundation for Animals (OFA) for clearance. All dogs certified as clear are assigned a certification number, which should appear on their pedigrees. Both hips are tested and scored individually; the lower the score, the less the degree of dysplasia. Clearly, dogs with evidence of dysplasia should not be incorporated into breeding programs.

SKIN PROBLEMS
A small percentage of SCWTs suffer from skin problems. These can be due to allergies, which are often difficult to determine, though allergy testing is available through one's vet. Correct diet can also help in keeping skin problems under control.

DO YOU KNOW ABOUT HIP DYSPLASIA?

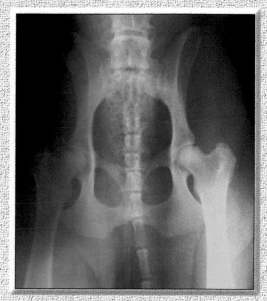

X-ray of a dog with "Good" hips.

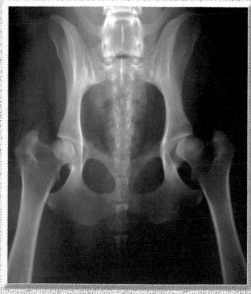

X-ray of a dog with "Moderate" dysplastic hips.

Hip dysplasia is a fairly common condition found in pure-bred dogs. When a dog has hip dysplasia, his hind leg has an incorrectly formed hip joint. By constant use of the hip joint, it becomes more and more loose, wears abnormally and may become arthritic.

Hip dysplasia can only be confirmed with an x-ray, but certain symptoms may indicate a problem. Your dog may have a hip dysplasia problem if he walks in a peculiar manner, hops instead of smoothly runs, uses his hind legs in unison (to keep the pressure off the weak joint), has trouble getting up from a prone position or always sits with both legs together on one side of his body.

As the dog matures, he may adapt well to life with a bad hip, but in a few years the arthritis develops and many dogs with hip dysplasia become crippled.

Hip dysplasia is considered an inherited disease and can be diagnosed definitively by x-ray only when the dog is two years old, although symptoms often appear earlier. Some experts claim that a special diet might help your puppy outgrow the bad hip, but the usual treatments are surgical. The removal of the pectineus muscle, the removal of the round part of the femur, reconstructing the pelvis and replacing the hip with an artificial one are all surgical interventions that are expensive, but they are usually very successful. Follow the advice of your veterinarian.

Named for his soft coat, this SCWT has the desirable abundant single coat that is soft in texture, silky with a gentle wave.

BREED STANDARD FOR THE

SOFT COATED WHEATEN TERRIER

INTRODUCTION TO THE BREED STANDARD

All breed standards are designed effectively to paint a picture in words, though each reader will almost certainly have a slightly different way of interpreting these words, just as a musical score is interpreted differently by different musicians. When all is said and done, were everyone to interpret a breed's standard in exactly the same way, there would only be one consistent winner within the breed at any given time!

The SCWT should be medium sized, well balanced and square in outline.

BREEDER'S BLUEPRINT

If you are considering breeding your bitch, it is very important that you are familiar with the breed standard. Reputable breeders breed with the intention of producing dogs that are as close as possible to the standard and that contribute to the advancement of the breed. Study the standard for both physical appearance and temperament, and make certain your bitch and your chosen stud dog measure up.

In any event, to fully comprehend the intricacies of a breed, reading words alone is never enough. In addition, it is essential also for devotees to watch Soft Coated Wheaten Terriers being judged at shows and, if possible, to attend seminars at which the breed is discussed. This enables owners and fanciers to absorb as much as possible about the breed that has captured their interest and admiration. "Hands-on" experience, providing an opportu-

However familiar one is with the Soft Coated Wheaten Terrier, it is always worth refreshing one's memory by re-reading the standard, for it is sometimes all too easy to overlook, or perhaps conveniently forget, certain features.

The breed standard for the Soft Coated Wheaten Terrier was written by the breed's parent club, the Soft Coated Wheaten Terrier Club of America, Inc. (SCWTCA), and was submitted and approved the American Kennel Club (AKC) in 1973. Since that time, the standard has been updated and reformatted, though its basic content remains essentially the same. The section on "General Appearance" does a fine job of summing up this handsome terrier breed, as does the section of "Temperament" give the reader an excellent overview of the breed's character.

nity to assess the structure of the dogs, is always valuable, especially for those who hope ultimately to judge the breed.

A breed standard undoubtedly helps breeders to produce stock that comes as close as possible to the recognized standard, and helps judges to know exactly what they are looking for. This enables a judge to make a carefully considered decision when selecting the most typical Soft Coated Wheaten Terrier present to head his line of winners.

AKC STANDARD FOR THE SOFT COATED WHEATEN TERRIER

General Appearance: The Soft Coated Wheaten Terrier is a medium-sized, hardy, well balanced sporting terrier, square in outline. He is distinguished by his soft, silky, gently waving coat of warm wheaten color and his particularly steady disposition. The breed requires moderation both in structure and presentation, and any exaggerations are to be shunned. He should present the overall appearance of an alert and happy animal, graceful, strong and well coordinated.

Size, Proportion, Substance: A dog shall be 18 to 19 inches at the withers, the ideal being 18.5. A bitch shall be 17 to 18 inches at the withers, the ideal being 17.5. *Major Faults*—Dogs under 18 inches or over 19 inches; bitches under 17 inches or over 18 inches. Any deviation must be penalized according to the degree of its severity. Square in outline. Hardy, well balanced. Dogs should weigh 35–40 pounds; bitches 30–35 pounds.

Head: Well balanced and in proportion to the body. Rectangular in appearance; moderately long. Powerful with no suggestion of coarseness. *Eyes* dark reddish brown or brown, medium in size, slightly almond shaped and set fairly wide apart. Eye rims black. *Major Fault*— Anything approaching a yellow eye. *Ears* small to medium in size, breaking level with the skull and dropping slightly forward, the inside edge of the ear lying next to the cheek and pointing to the ground rather than to the eye. A hound ear or a high-breaking ear is not typical and should be *severely penalized*. *Skull* flat and clean between ears. Cheekbones not prominent. Defined stop. *Muzzle* powerful and strong, well filled below the eyes. No suggestion of snipiness. Skull and

The gait or movement of the SCWT should be free, graceful and lively, accomplished by long, low strides.

LEFT: The old-fashioned, untrimmed working farm-dog type of SCWT with wavy, silky coat. RIGHT: The modern SCWT type with moderate grooming style and heavier coat.

foreface of equal length. *Nose* black and large for size of dog. *Major Fault*—Any nose color other than solid black. *Lips* tight and black. *Teeth* large, clean and white; scissors or level bite. *Major Fault*—Undershot or overshot.

Neck, Topline, Body: *Neck* medium in length, clean and strong, not throaty. Carried proudly, it gradually widens, blending smoothly into the body. *Back* strong and level. *Body* compact; relatively short coupled. *Chest* is deep. *Ribs* are well sprung but without roundness. *Tail* is docked and well set on, carried gaily but never over the back.

Forequarters: *Shoulders* well laid back, clean and smooth; well knit.

Forelegs straight and well boned. All *dewclaws* should be removed. *Feet* are round and compact with good depth of pad. *Pads* black. *Nails* dark.

Hindquarters: *Hind* legs well developed with well bent *stifles* turning neither in nor out; *hocks* well let down and parallel to each other. All *dewclaws* should be removed. The presence of dewclaws on the hind legs should be *penalized*. *Feet* are round and compact with good depth of pad. *Pads* black. *Nails* dark.

Coat: A distinguishing characteristic of the breed which sets the dog apart from all other terriers. An abundant single coat covering the entire body, legs and head; coat on the latter falls forward to shade the eyes. Texture soft and silky with a gentle wave. In both puppies and adolescents, the mature wavy coat is generally not yet evident. *Major Faults*— Woolly or harsh, crisp or cottony, curly or standaway coat; in the adult, a straight coat is also objectionable.

Presentation—For show purposes, the Wheaten is presented to show a terrier outline, but coat must be of sufficient length to flow when the dog is in motion. The coat must never be clipped or plucked. Sharp contrasts or stylizations must be avoided. Head coat should be blended to present a rectangular outline. Eyes should be indicated but never fully exposed. Ears should be relieved of fringe, but not taken down to the leather. Sufficient coat must be left on skull, cheeks, neck and tail to balance the proper length of body coat. Dogs that are overly trimmed shall be severely penalized.

Color: Any shade of wheaten. Upon close examination, occasional red, white or black guard hairs may be found. However, the overall coloring must be clearly wheaten with no evidence of any other color except on ears and muzzle where blue-gray shading is sometimes present. *Major Fault*—Any color save wheaten. *Puppies* and *Adolescents*—Puppies under a

SCWT profile shows incorrect bushy stand-off coat without shine, wave or flow. The coat should be neither cottony nor excessively curly (like a Kerry Blue Terrier).

The "Irish" coat is finer and silkier, usually with varying degrees of wave, neither as dense nor as long as modern coats, particularly on the legs.

year may carry deeper coloring and occasional black tipping. The adolescent, under two years, is often quite light in color, but

Modern-type SCWT with moderate terrier trim and correct coat with slight wave, shine and flow. This figure shows the correct proportion and balance.

The show judge reviews each SCWT in the lineup, evaluating its positive features and flaws.

Each dog is compared to the perfect dog described in the breed standard. The SCWT that most closely conforms, in the judge's opinion, is selected as Best of Breed.

must never be white or carry gray other than on ears and muzzle. However, by two years of age, the *proper* wheaten color should be obvious.

Gait: Gait is free, graceful and lively with good reach in front and strong drive behind. Front and rear feet turn neither in nor out. Dogs who fail to keep their tails erect when moving should be *severely penalized.*

Temperament: The Wheaten is a happy, steady dog and shows himself gaily with an air of self-confidence. He is alert and exhibits interest in his surroundings; exhibits less aggressiveness than is sometimes encouraged in

FAULTS IN THE SCWT

Weak, under-developed rear, straight in rear with low tailset. Straight front, which can be seen even in a coated breed because the front legs are under the body.

An extreme grooming style that finds favor in some circles, but is incorrect. Note "conehead" and over-angulated rear.

Short neck, sloping topline; over-angulated rear with gay tail; a bit low on leg.

Long back, low tail set, straight in rear.

other terriers. *Major Fault*—Timid or overly aggressive dogs.

Approved February 12, 1983
Reformatted July 20, 1989

The SCWT's gait should be strong and lively.

Without helpful information and sound advice, new puppy owners may find themselves up a tree when it comes to choosing the best SCWT for them.

SOFT COATED WHEATEN TERRIER

WHERE TO BEGIN

Before reaching the decision that you will begin your search for a Soft Coated Wheaten Terrier puppy, it is essential that you are really sure that this is the most suitable breed for you and for your family. You should have carefully researched the breed before making your decision, weighing all the pros and cons against each other, before reaching your final conclusion that this is truly the breed with which you want to share your lives.

When you have made that decision, you must also ask yourself why you want a Soft Coated Wheaten Terrier. Do you want a SCWT purely as a pet or as a show dog? This should be made clear to the breeder when you make your initial inquiries, for you will need to take the breeder's advice as to which available puppy will be best suited to you; for example, which one shows the most promise for the show ring. If looking for a pet, you should have discussed your family situation with the breeder, and again taken

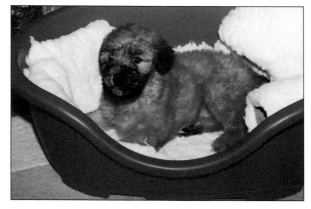

advice as to which puppy is likely to suit best.

When you have your first opportunity to visit the most potentially suitable litter, watch the puppies interact together. You will find that different puppies have different personalities and that some will be more boisterous and extroverted than others. You should expect the puppies to come to you even if they don't know you, so don't take pity on the unduly shy puppy that sits quietly in a corner. Although you will need to use your own judgment as to which one is most likely to fit in with your own

Making your Wheaten puppy feel at home will take preparation, time and money on your part.

PEDIGREE VS. REGISTRATION CERTIFICATE

Too often new owners are confused between these two important documents. Your puppy's pedigree, essentially a family tree, is a written record of a dog's genealogy of three generations or more. The pedigree will show you the names as well as performance titles of all dogs in your pup's background. Your breeder must provide you with a registration application, with his part properly filled out. You must complete the application and send it to the AKC with the proper fee. Every puppy must come from a litter that has been AKC-registered by the breeder, born in the USA and from a sire and dam that are also registered with the AKC.

The seller must provide you with complete records to identify the puppy. The AKC requires that the seller provide the buyer with the following: breed; sex, color and markings; date of birth; litter number (when available); names and registration numbers of the parents; breeder's name; and date sold or delivered.

giving you an opportunity to see the breed in some numbers. This will have provided you with a chance to see the dogs with their breeders and owners.

Remember that the dog you select should remain with you for the duration of his life, which will hopefully be somewhere between 12 and 15 years, so making the right decision from the outset is of utmost importance. No dog should be moved from one home to another simply because his owners were not considerate enough to have done sufficient research before selecting the breed. It is always important to remember that when you are looking for a puppy, a good breeder will be assessing

lifestyle, if the breeder you have selected is a good one, you will also be guided by his or her judgment and knowledge.

You should have done plenty of background "homework" on the breed, and preferably have visited a specialty or all-breed show,

you as a prospective new owner just as carefully as you are selecting the breeder.

Puppies almost invariably look enchanting, but you must select one from a caring breeder who has given the puppies all the attention they have deserved and has looked after them well. The puppy you select should look well fed, but not pot-bellied, as this might indicate worms. Eyes should look bright and clear, without discharge. The nose should be moist, an indication of good health, but should never be runny. It goes without saying that there should certainly be no evidence of loose bowels or of parasites. The puppy you choose

PET INSURANCE

Just as you can insure your car, your house and your own health, you likewise can insure your dog's health. Investigate a pet insurance policy by talking to your vet. Depending on the age of your dog, the breed and the kind of coverage you desire, your policy can be very affordable. Most policies cover accidental injuries, poisoning and thousands of medical problems and illnesses, including cancers. Some carriers also offer routine care and immunization coverage.

should also have a healthy-looking coat, an important indication of good health internally. Always check the bite of your selected puppy to be sure that it is neither overshot nor undershot. This may not be too noticeable on a young puppy, but will become more evident as the puppy gets older.

Sex may play a part in your selection of a SCWT puppy. Do you want a male or a female? The main difference between males and females in this breed is that males are generally bigger and more heavily set.

Something else to consider is whether or not to take out veterinary insurance. Insurance for pets is fast becoming very common in the US and is quite affordable. Vets' bills can mount up, and you

Meeting the litter is an exciting prospect, and necessary to make the right selection. The litter should be lively, appear healthy and be interested in your visit.

must always be certain that sufficient funds are available to give your dog any veterinary attention that may be needed. Depending on the policy you select, routine veterinary checkups may be included.

FINDING A BREEDER AND PUPPY

If you are convinced that the Soft Coated Wheaten Terrier is the ideal dog for you, it's time to learn about where to find a puppy and what to look for. Locating a litter of SCWTs should not present a problem for the new owner. You should inquire about breeders in your area who enjoy a good reputation in the breed. You are looking for an established breeder with outstanding dog ethics and a strong commitment to the breed. He, no doubt, is an active member of the SCWTCA and shows his dogs. New owners should have as many questions as they have doubts. An established breeder is indeed the one to answer your four million questions and make you comfortable with your choice of the Soft Coated Wheaten Terrier. An established breeder will sell you a puppy at a fair price if, and only if, the breeder determines that you are a suitably worthy owner of his dogs. An established breeder can be relied upon for advice, no matter what time of day or night. A reputable breeder

will accept a puppy back, should you decide that this is not the right dog for you.

When choosing a breeder, reputation is much more important than convenience of location. Do not be overly impressed by breeders who run brag advertisements in the show

A SHOW PUPPY

If you plan to show your puppy, you must first deal with a reputable breeder who shows his dogs and has had some success in the conformation ring. The puppy's pedigree should include one or more champions in the first and second generation. You should be familiar with the breed and breed standard so you can know what qualities to look for in your puppy. The breeder's observations and recommendations also are invaluable aids in selecting your future champion. If you consider an older puppy, be sure that the puppy has been properly socialized with people and not isolated in a kennel without substantial daily human contact.

programs about their stupendous champions. Many quality breeders are quiet and unassuming. You hear about them at the dog shows, by word of mouth. You may be well advised to avoid the novice who lives only a few miles away. The novice breeder, trying so hard to get rid of that first litter of puppies, is more than accommodating and anxious to sell you one. That breeder will charge you as much as any established breeder. The novice breeder isn't going to interrogate you and your family about your intentions with the puppy, the environment and training you can provide, etc. That breeder will be nowhere to be found when your poorly bred, badly adjusted four-pawed monster starts to growl and spit up at midnight or eat the family cat!

Choosing a breeder is an important first step in dog ownership. Fortunately, the majority of SCWT breeders are devoted to the breed and its well-being. New owners should have little problem finding a reputable breeder who doesn't live on the other side of the country. The American Kennel Club is able to recommend breeders of quality SCWTs, as can the SCWTCA's breeder list.

Once you have contacted and met a breeder or two and made your choice about which breeder is best suited to your needs, it's

SIGNS OF A HEALTHY PUPPY
Healthy puppies are robust little fellows who are alert and active, sporting shiny coats and supple skin. They should not appear lethargic, bloated or pot-bellied, nor should they have flaky skin or runny or crusted eyes or noses. Their stools should be firm and well formed, with no evidence of blood or mucus.

time to visit the litter. Keep in mind that many top breeders have waiting lists. Sometimes new owners have to wait as long as two years for a puppy. If you are really committed to the breeder whom you've selected, then you will wait (and hope for an early arrival!). If not, you may have to

NEW RELEASES

Most breeders release their puppies between eight and ten weeks of age. A breeder who allows puppies to leave the litter at five or six weeks of age may be more concerned with profit than with the puppies' welfare. However, some breeders of show or working breeds may hold one or more top-quality puppies longer, occasionally until three or four months of age, in order to evaluate the puppies' career or show potential and decide which one(s) they will keep for themselves.

and not a show dog, you simply should select a pup that is friendly, attractive and healthy. Soft Coated Wheaten Terriers generally have litters averaging six puppies, so you will have a selection of pups from which to choose once you have located a desirable litter.

Breeders commonly allow visitors to see their litters by around the fifth or sixth week, and puppies leave for their new homes between the eighth and tenth week. Breeders who permit their puppies to leave early are more interested in your money than in their puppies' well-being. Puppies need to learn the rules of the pack from their dams, and most dams continue teaching the pups manners and dos and don'ts until around the eighth week. Breeders spend significant amounts of time with the SCWT toddlers so that the pups are able to interact with the "other species," i.e., humans. Given the long history that dogs and humans have, bonding between the two species is natural but must be nurtured. A well-bred, well-socialized Wheaten pup wants nothing more than to be near you and please you.

A COMMITTED NEW OWNER

By now you should understand what makes the SCWT a most unique and special dog, one that will fit nicely into your family

go with your second- or third-choice breeder. Don't be too anxious, however. If the breeder doesn't have a waiting list, or any customers, there is probably a good reason.

Since you are likely to be choosing a Wheaten as a pet dog

and lifestyle. If you have researched breeders, you should be able to recognize a knowledgeable and responsible SCWT breeder who cares not only about his pups but also about what kind of owner you will be. If you have completed the final step in your new journey, you have found a litter, or possibly two, of quality SCWT pups.

A visit with the puppies and their breeder should be an education in itself. Breed research, breeder selection and puppy visitation are very important aspects of finding the puppy of your dreams. Beyond that, these things also lay the foundation for a successful future with your pup. Puppy personalities within each litter vary, from the shy and easygoing puppy to the one who is dominant and assertive, with most pups falling somewhere in between. By spending time with the puppies, you will be able to recognize certain behaviors and what these behaviors indicate about each pup's temperament. Which type of pup will complement your family dynamics is best determined by observing the puppies in action within their "pack." Your breeder's expertise and recommendations are also valuable. Although you may fall in love with a bold and brassy male, the breeder may suggest that another pup would be best for

you. The breeder's experience in rearing SCWT pups and matching their temperaments with appropriate humans offers the best assurance that your pup will meet your needs and expectations. The type of puppy that you select is just as important as your decision that the SCWT is the breed for you.

The decision to live with a SCWT is a serious commitment and not one to be taken lightly. This puppy is a living sentient being that will be dependent on you for basic survival for his entire life. Beyond the basics of survival—food, water, shelter and protection—he needs much, much more. The new pup needs love, nurturing and a proper canine education to mold him into a responsible, well-behaved canine citizen. Your SCWT's health and good manners will need consistent monitoring and regular "tune-ups," so your job as a responsible

The breeder should provide you with a sample of the puppy's food as well as an instruction sheet that outlines the diet and other basic rearing guidelines.

HOUSE-TRAINING SIGNALS

Watch your puppy for signs that he has to relieve himself (sniffing, circling and squatting), and waste no time in whisking him outside to do his business. Once the puppy is older, you should attach his leash and head for the door. Puppies will always "go" immediately after they wake up, within minutes after eating and after brief periods of play, but young puppies should also be taken out regularly at times other than these, just in case! If necessary, set a timer to remind you to take him out.

dog owner will be ongoing throughout every stage of his life. If you are not prepared to accept these responsibilities and commit to them for the next decade, likely longer, then you are not prepared to own a dog of any breed.

Although the responsibilities of owning a dog may at times tax your patience, the joy of living with your SCWT far outweighs the workload, and a well-mannered adult dog is worth your time and effort. Before your very eyes, your new charge will grow up to be your most loyal friend, devoted to you unconditionally.

YOUR SCWT SHOPPING LIST

Just as expectant parents prepare a nursery for their baby, so should you ready your home for the arrival of your SCWT pup. If you have the necessary puppy supplies purchased and in place before he comes home, it will ease the puppy's transition from the warmth and familiarity of his mom and littermates to the brand-new environment of his new home and human family. You will be too busy to stock up and prepare your house after your pup comes home, that's for sure! Imagine how a pup must feel upon being transported to a strange new place. It's up to you to comfort him and to let your little pup know that he is going to be happy with you.

FOOD AND WATER BOWLS

Your puppy will need separate bowls for his food and water. Stainless steel pans are generally preferred over plastic bowls since they sterilize better and pups are less inclined to chew on the metal. Heavy-duty ceramic bowls are popular, but consider how often you will have to pick up those heavy bowls. Buy adult-sized pans, as your puppy will grow into them before you know it.

THE DOG CRATE

If you think that crates are tools of punishment and confinement for when a dog has misbehaved, think again. Most breeders and almost all trainers recommend a crate as the preferred house-training aid as well as for all-around puppy training and safety. Because dogs are natural den creatures that prefer cave-like environments, the benefits of crate use are many. The crate provides the puppy with his very own "safe house," a cozy place to sleep, take a break or seek comfort with a favorite toy; a travel aid to house your dog when on the road, at motels or at the vet's office; a training aid to help teach your puppy proper toileting habits; a place of solitude when non-dog people happen to drop by and don't want a lively puppy—or even a well-behaved adult dog—saying hello or begging for attention.

Crates come in several types, although the wire crate and the fiberglass airline-type crate are the most popular. Both are safe, and your puppy will adjust to either one, so the choice is up to you. The wire crates offer better visibility for the pup as well as better ventilation. Many of the wire crates easily collapse into suitcase-size carriers. The

fiberglass crates, similar to those used by the airlines for animal transport, are sturdier and more den-like. However, the fiberglass crates do not collapse and are less ventilated than a wire crate, which can be problematic in hot weather. Some of the newer crates are made of heavy plastic mesh; they are very lightweight and fold up into slim-line suitcases. However, a mesh crate might not be suitable for a pup with manic chewing habits.

Don't bother with a puppy-sized crate. Although your SCWT will be a wee fellow when you bring him home, he will grow up in the blink of an eye and your puppy crate will be useless. Purchase a crate that will accommodate an adult SCWT. He will stand about 19 inches at the shoulder, so a medium- to large-sized crate will fit him nicely.

BEDDING AND CRATE PADS

Your puppy will enjoy some type of soft bedding in his "room" (the crate), something he can snuggle into to feel cozy and secure. Old towels or blankets are good choices for a young pup, since he may (and probably will) have a toileting accident or two in the crate or decide to chew on the bedding material. Once he is fully trained and out of the early chewing stage, you can replace the puppy bedding with a permanent crate pad if you prefer. Crate pads

Your local pet
shop should have
a wide array of
dog crates
available.
Purchase a large
enough crate so
that your SCWT
will fit as an
adult too.

and other dog beds run the gamut
from inexpensive to high-end
doggie-designer styles, but don't
splurge on the good stuff until
you are sure that your puppy is
reliable and won't tear it up or
make a mess on it.

PUPPY TOYS

Just as infants and older children
require objects to stimulate their
minds and bodies, puppies need
toys to entertain their curious
brains, wiggly paws and achy
teeth. A fun array of safe doggie
toys will help satisfy your
puppy's chewing instincts and
distract him from gnawing on the
leg of your antique chair or your
new leather sofa. Most puppy toys
are cute and look as if they would
be a lot of fun, but not all are

necessarily safe or good for your
puppy, so use caution when you
go puppy-toy shopping.

Although SCWT's are not
known to be voracious chewers
like many other dogs, they still
love to chew. The best "chewci-
fiers" are nylon and hard rubber
bones, which are safe to gnaw on
and come in sizes appropriate for
all age groups and breeds. Be
especially careful of natural
bones, which can splinter or
develop dangerous sharp edges;
pups can easily swallow or choke
on those bone splinters.
Veterinarians often tell of surgical
nightmares involving bits of
splintered bone, because in
addition to the danger of choking,
the sharp pieces can damage the
intestinal tract.

Similarly, rawhide chews,
while a favorite of most dogs and
puppies, can be equally
dangerous. Pieces of rawhide are
easily swallowed after they get all
gummy from chewing, and dogs
have been known to choke on
large pieces of ingested rawhide.
Rawhide chews should be offered
only when you can supervise the
puppy.

Soft woolly toys are special
puppy favorites. They come in a
wide variety of cute shapes and
sizes; some look like little stuffed
animals. Puppies love to shake
them up and toss them about, or
simply carry them around. Be
careful of fuzzy toys that have

button eyes or noses that your pup could chew off and swallow, and make sure that he does not disembowel a squeaky toy to remove the squeaker! Braided rope toys are similar in that they are fun to chew and toss around, but they shred easily and the strings are easy to swallow. The strings are not digestible and, if the puppy doesn't pass them in his stool, he could end up at the vet's office. As with rawhides, your puppy should be closely monitored with rope toys.

If you believe that your pup has ingested one of these forbidden objects, check his stools for the next couple of days to see if he passes the object when he defecates. At the same time, also watch for signs of intestinal distress. A call to your veterinarian might be in order to get his advice and be on the safe side.

An all-time favorite toy for puppies (young and old!) is the empty gallon milk jug. Hard plastic juice containers—46

TOYS 'R SAFE

The vast array of tantalizing puppy toys is staggering. Stroll through any pet shop or pet-supply outlet and you will see that the choices can be overwhelming. However, not all dog toys are safe or sensible. Most very young puppies enjoy soft woolly toys that they can snuggle with and carry

around. (You know they have outgrown them when they shred them up!) Avoid toys that have buttons, tabs or other enhancements that can be chewed off and swallowed. Soft toys that squeak are fun, but make sure your puppy does not disembowel the toy and remove (and swallow) the squeaker. Toys that rattle or make noise can excite a puppy, but they present the same danger as the squeaky kind and so require supervision. Hard rubber toys that bounce can also entertain a pup, but make sure that the toy is too big for your pup to swallow.

Soft cozy bedding in your Softie's crate will make him feel right at home. Make sure the bedding is machine-washable and durable since accidents will happen.

ounces or more—are also excellent. Such containers make lots of noise when they are batted about, and puppies go crazy with

MAKE A COMMITMENT

Dogs are most assuredly man's best friend, but they are also a lot of work. When you add a puppy to your family, you also are adding to your daily responsibilities for years to come. Dogs need more than just food, water and a place to sleep. They also require training (which can be ongoing throughout the lifetime of the dog), activity to keep him physically and mentally fit and hands-on attention every day, plus grooming and health care. Your life as you now know it may well disappear! Are you prepared for such drastic changes?

delight as they play with them. However, they don't often last very long, so be sure to remove and replace them when they get chewed up on the ends.

A word of caution about homemade toys: be careful with your choices of non-traditional play objects. Never use old shoes or socks, since a puppy cannot distinguish between the old ones on which he's allowed to chew and the new ones in your closet that are strictly off limits. That principle applies to anything that resembles something that you don't want your puppy to chew up.

COLLARS

A lightweight nylon collar is the best choice for a very young pup. Quick-clip collars are easy to put on and remove, and they can be adjusted as the puppy grows. Introduce him to his collar as soon as he comes home to get him accustomed to wearing it. He'll get used to it quickly and won't mind a bit. Make sure that it is snug enough that it won't slip off, yet loose enough to be comfortable for the pup. You should be able to slip two fingers between the collar and his neck. Check the collar often, as puppies grow in spurts, and his collar can become too tight almost overnight. Choke collars are for training purposes only and should never be used on a puppy under five months old.

COLLARING OUR CANINES

The standard flat collar with a buckle or a snap, in leather, nylon or cotton, is widely regarded as the everyday all-purpose collar. If the collar fits correctly, you should be able to fit two fingers between the collar and the dog's neck.

Leather Buckle Collars

Limited-Slip Collar

The martingale, Greyhound or limited-slip collar is preferred by many dog owners and trainers. It is fixed with an extra loop that tightens when pressure is applied to the leash. The martingale collar gets tighter but does not "choke" the dog. The limited-slip collar should only be used for walking and training, not for free play or interaction with another dog. These types of collar should never be left on the dog, as the extra loop can lead to accidents.

Choke collars, usually made of stainless steel, are made for training purposes, but are not recommended for small dogs or heavily coated breeds. The chains can injure small dogs or damage long/abundant coats. Thin nylon choke leads are commonly used on show dogs while in the ring, though they are not practical for everyday use.

Snap Bolt Choke Collar

The harness, with two or three straps that attach over the dog's shoulders and around his torso, is a humane and safe alternative to the conventional collar. By and large, a well-made harness is virtually escape-proof. Harnesses are available in nylon and mesh and can be outfitted on most dogs, ranging from chest girths of 10 to 30 inches.

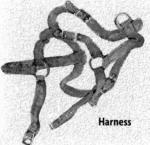

Harness

Nylon Collar

Quick-Click Closure

Snake Chain

Chrome Steel

Fur-Saver

Choke Chain Collars

A head collar, composed of a nylon strap that goes around the dog's muzzle and a second strap that wraps around his neck, offers the owner better control over his dog. This device is recommended for problem-solving with dogs (including jumping up, pulling and aggressive behaviors), but must be used with care.

A training halter, including a flat collar and two straps, made of nylon and webbing, is designed for walking. There are several on the market; some are more difficult to put on the dog than others. The halter harness, with two small slip rings at each end, is recommended for ease of use.

TEETHING TIME

All puppies chew. It's normal canine behavior. Chewing just plain feels good to a puppy, especially during the three- to five-month teething period when the adult teeth are breaking through the gums. Rather than attempting to eliminate such a strong natural chewing instinct, you will be more successful if you redirect it and teach your puppy what he may or may not chew. Correct inappropriate chewing with a sharp "No!" and offer him a chew toy, praising him when he takes it. Don't become discouraged. Chewing usually decreases after the adult teeth have come in.

LEASHES

A 6-foot nylon lead is an excellent choice for a young puppy. It is lightweight and not as tempting to chew as a leather lead. You can switch to a 6-foot leather lead after your pup has grown and is used to walking politely on a lead. For initial puppy walks and house-training purposes, you should invest in a shorter lead so that you have more control over the puppy. At first, you don't want him wandering too far away from you, and when taking him out for toileting you will want to keep him in the specific area chosen for his potty spot.

Once the puppy is heel trained with a traditional leash, you can consider purchasing a retractable lead. A retractable lead is excellent for walking adult dogs that are already leash-wise. The retractable lead allows the dog to roam farther away from you and explore a wider area when out walking, and also retracts when you need to keep him close to you.

HOME SAFETY FOR YOUR PUPPY

The importance of puppy-proofing cannot be overstated. In addition to making your house comfortable for your SCWT's arrival, you also must make sure that your house is safe for your puppy before you bring him home. There are countless hazards in the owner's personal living environment that a pup can sniff, chew, swallow or destroy. Many are obvious; others are not. Do a thorough advance house check to remove or rearrange those things that could hurt your puppy, keeping any potentially dangerous items out of areas to which he will have access.

LEASH LIFE

Dogs love leashes! Believe it or not, most dogs dance for joy every time their owners pick up their leashes. The leash means that the dog is going for a walk—and there are few things more exciting than that! Here are some of the kinds of leashes that are commercially available.

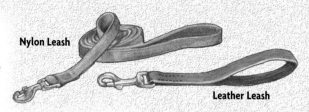

Nylon Leash

Leather Leash

Traditional Leash: Made of cotton, nylon or leather, these leashes are usually about 6 feet in length. A quality-made leather leash is softer on the hands than a nylon one. Durable woven cotton is a popular option. Lengths can vary up to about 48 feet, designed for different uses.

Chain Leash: Usually a metal chain leash with a plastic handle. This is not the best choice for most breeds, as it is heavier than other leashes and difficult to manage.

Retractable Leash: A long nylon cord is housed in a plastic device for extending and retracting. This leash, also known as a flexible leash, is ideal for taking trained dogs for long walks in open areas, although it is not recommended for large, powerful breeds. Different lengths and sizes are available, so check that you purchase one appropriate for your dog's weight.

Elastic Leash: A nylon leash with an elastic extension. This is useful for well-trained dogs, especially in conjunction with a head halter.

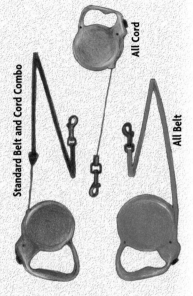

Retractable Leashes

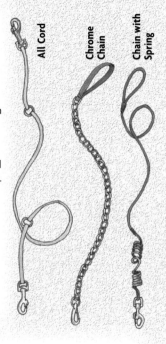

Avoid leashes that are completely elastic, as they afford minimal control to the handler.

Adjustable Leash: This has two snaps, one on each end, and several metal rings. It is handy if you need to tether your dog temporarily, but is never to be used with a choke collar.

Tab Leash: A short leash (4 to 6 inches long) that attaches to your dog's collar. This device serves like a handle, in case you have to grab your dog while he's exercising off lead. It's ideal for "half-trained" dogs or dogs that only listen half the time.

Slip Leash: Essentially a leash with a collar built in, similar to what a dog-show handler uses to show a dog. This British-style collar has a ring on the end so that you can form a slip collar. Useful if you have to catch your own runaway dog or a stray.

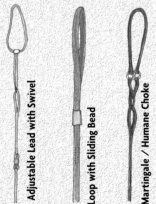

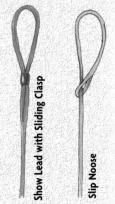

A Variety of Collar-and-Leash-in-One Products

Electrical cords are especially dangerous, since puppies view them as irresistible chew toys. Unplug and remove all exposed cords or fasten them beneath a baseboard where the puppy cannot reach them. Veterinarians and firefighters can tell you horror stories about electrical burns and house fires that resulted from puppy-chewed electrical cords. Consider this a most serious precaution for your puppy and the rest of your family.

Scout your home for tiny objects that might be seen at a pup's eye level. Keep medication bottles and cleaning supplies well out of reach, and do the same with waste baskets and other trash containers. It goes without saying that you should not use rodent poison or other toxic chemicals in any puppy area and that you must keep such containers safely locked up. You will be amazed at how many places a curious puppy can discover.

Once your house has cleared inspection, check your yard. A sturdy fence, well embedded into the ground, will give your dog a safe place to play and potty. All terriers are prone to dig, and the SCWT is no exception, though he's not as avid a digger as his short-legged brethren. Although SCWTs are not known to be climbers or fence jumpers, they are still athletic dogs, so a 5- to 6-foot-high fence should be adequate to contain an agile youngster or adult. Check the fence periodically for necessary repairs. If there is a weak link or space to squeeze through, you can be sure a determined SCWT will discover it.

The garage and shed can be hazardous places for a pup, as things like fertilizers, chemicals and tools are usually kept there. It's best to keep these areas off limits to the pup. Antifreeze is especially dangerous to dogs, as they find the taste appealing and it takes only a few licks from the driveway to kill a dog, puppy or adult, small breed or large.

CREATE A SCHEDULE

Puppies thrive on sameness and routine. Offer meals at the same time each day, take him out at regular times for potty trips and do the same for play periods and outdoor activity. Make note of when your puppy naps and when he is most lively and energetic, and try to plan his day around those times. Once he is house-trained and more predictable in his habits, he will be better able to tolerate changes in his schedule.

VISITING THE VETERINARIAN
A good veterinarian is your SCWT puppy's best health-insurance policy. If you do not already have a vet, ask friends and experienced dog people in your area for recommendations so that you can

select a vet before you bring your SCWT puppy home. Also arrange for your puppy's first veterinary examination beforehand, since many vets have waiting periods for appointments, and your puppy should visit the vet within a day or so of coming home.

It's important to make sure your puppy's first visit to the vet is a pleasant and positive one. The vet should take great care to befriend the pup and handle him gently to make their first meeting a positive experience. The vet will give the pup a thorough physical examination and set up a schedule for vaccinations and

It is your responsibility to clean up after your dog has relieved himself. Pet shops sell various aids to assist in the clean-up task.

other necessary wellness visits. Be sure to show your vet any health and inoculation records, which you should have received from your breeder. Your vet is a great source of canine health information, so be sure to ask questions and take notes. Creating a health journal for your puppy will make a handy reference for his wellness and any future health problems that may arise.

ARE VACCINATIONS NECESSARY?

Vaccinations are recommended for all puppies by the American Veterinary Medical Association (AVMA). Some vaccines are absolutely necessary, while others depend upon a dog's or puppy's individual exposure to certain diseases or the animal's immune history. Rabies vaccinations are required by law in all 50 states. Some diseases are fatal whereas others are treatable, making the need for vaccinating against the latter questionable. Follow your veterinarian's recommendations to keep your dog fully immunized and protected. You can also review the AVMA directive on vaccinations on their website: www.avma.org.

All puppies are orally obsessed and will chew and bite at anything that feels good. Owners must direct the puppy's chewing from the outset to keep problems from developing.

MEETING THE FAMILY

Your SCWT's homecoming is an exciting time for all members of the family, and it's only natural that everyone will be eager to meet him, pet him and play with him. However, for the puppy's sake, it's best to make these initial family meetings as uneventful as possible so that the pup is not overwhelmed with too much too soon. Remember, he has just left his dam and his littermates and is away from the breeder's home for the first time. Despite his fuzzy wagging tail, he is still apprehensive and wondering where he is and who all these strange humans are. It's best to let him explore on his own and meet the family members as he feels comfortable. Let him investigate all the new smells, sights and sounds at his own pace. Children should be especially careful to not get overly excited, use loud voices or hug the pup too tightly. Be calm, gentle and affectionate, and be ready to comfort him if he appears frightened or uneasy.

Be sure to show your puppy his new crate during this first day home. Toss a treat or two inside the crate; if he associates the crate with food, he will associate the crate with good things. If he is comfortable with the crate, you can offer him his first meal inside it. Leave the door ajar so he can wander in and out as he chooses.

FIRST NIGHT IN HIS NEW HOME

So much has happened in your SCWT puppy's first day away from the breeder. He's had his first car ride to his new home. He's met his new human family and perhaps the other family pets. He has explored his new house and yard, at least those places where he is to be allowed during his first weeks at home. He may have visited his new veterinarian. He has eaten his first meal or two away from his dam and littermates. Surely that's enough to tire out an eight-week-old SCWT pup...or so you hope!

It's bedtime. During the day, the pup investigated his crate, which is his new den and sleeping space, so it is not entirely strange to him. Line the crate with

a soft towel or blanket that he can snuggle into and gently place him into the crate for the night. Some breeders send home a piece of bedding from where the pup slept with his littermates, and those familiar scents are a great comfort for the puppy on his first night without his siblings.

He will probably whine or cry. The puppy is objecting to the confinement and the fact that he is alone for the first time. This can be a stressful time for you as well as for the pup. It's important that you remain strong and don't let the puppy out of his crate to comfort him. He will fall asleep eventually. If you release him, the puppy will learn that crying means "out" and will continue that habit. You are laying the groundwork for future habits.

FIRST CAR RIDE
The ride to your home from the breeder will no doubt be your puppy's first automobile experience, and you should make every effort to keep him comfortable and secure. Bring a large towel or small blanket for the puppy to lie on during the trip and an extra towel in case the pup gets carsick or has a potty accident. It's best to have another person with you to hold the puppy in his lap. Most puppies will fall fast asleep from the rolling motion of the car. If the ride is lengthy, you may have to stop so that the puppy can relieve himself, so be sure to bring a leash and collar for those stops. Avoid rest areas for potty trips, since those are frequented by many dogs, who may carry parasites or disease. It's better to stop at grassy areas near gas stations or shopping centers to prevent unhealthy exposure for your pup.

Allow your new SCWT puppy to acclimate himself to your home and yard. In little time, the puppy will begin to feel at home.

Some breeders find that soft music can soothe a crying pup and help him get to sleep.

SOCIALIZING YOUR PUPPY
The first 20 weeks of your SCWT puppy's life are the most important of his entire lifetime. A properly socialized puppy will grow up to be a confident and stable adult who will be a pleasure to live with and a welcome addition to the neighborhood.

WATCH THE WATER
To help your puppy sleep through the night without having to relieve himself, remove his water bowl after 7 p.m. Offer him a couple of ice cubes during the evening to quench his thirst. Never leave water in a puppy's crate, as this is inviting puddles of mishaps.

The importance of socialization cannot be overemphasized. Research on canine behavior has proven that puppies who are not exposed to new sights, sounds, people and animals during their first 20 weeks of life will grow up to be timid and fearful, even aggressive, and unable to flourish outside of their familiar home environment.

Socializing your puppy is not difficult and, in fact, will be a fun time for you both. Lead training goes hand in hand with socialization, so your puppy will be learning how to walk on a lead at the same time that he's meeting the neighborhood. Because the SCWT is a such a terrific breed, your puppy will enjoy being "the new kid on the block." Take him for short walks, to the park and to other dog-friendly places where he will encounter new people, especially children. Puppies automatically recognize children as "little people" and are drawn to play with them. Just make sure that you supervise these meetings and that the children do not get too rough or encourage him to play too hard. An overzealous pup can often nip too hard, frightening the child and in turn making the puppy overly excited. A bad experience in puppyhood can impact a dog for life, so a pup that has a negative experience with a child may grow up to be shy or even aggressive around children.

Take your puppy along on your daily errands. Puppies are natural "people magnets," and most people who see your pup will want to pet him. All of these encounters will help to mold him into a confident adult dog. Likewise, you will soon feel like a confident, responsible dog owner, rightly proud of your handsome SCWT.

Be especially careful of your puppy's encounters and experiences during the eight-to-ten-week-old period, which is also called the "fear period." This is a serious imprinting period, and all contact during this time should be gentle and positive. A frightening or negative event could leave a permanent impression that could affect his future behavior if a similar situation arises.

Also make sure that your puppy has received his first and second rounds of vaccinations before you expose him to other dogs or bring him to places that other dogs may frequent. Avoid dog parks and other strange-dog areas until your vet assures you that your puppy is fully immunized and resistant to the diseases that can be passed between canines. Discuss socialization with your breeder, as some breeders recommend socializing the puppy even before he has received all of his inoculations, depending on how outgoing the breed or puppy may be.

LEADER OF THE PUPPY'S PACK

Like other canines, your puppy needs an authority figure, someone he can look up to and regard as the leader of his "pack." His first pack leader was his dam, who taught him to be polite and not chew too hard on her ears or nip at her muzzle. He learned those same lessons from his litter-mates. If he played too rough,

MEET THE PARENTS
Because puppies are a combination of genes inherited from both of their parents, they will reflect the qualities and temperament of their sire and dam. When visiting a litter of pups, spend time with the dam and observe her behavior with her puppies, the breeder and with strangers. The sire is often not on the premises, but the dam should be with her pups until they are about eight weeks old. If either parent is surly, quarrelsome or fearful, it's likely that some of the pups will inherit those tendencies.

they cried in pain and stopped the game, which sent an important message to the rowdy puppy.

As puppies play together, they are also struggling to determine who will be the boss. Being pack animals, dogs need someone to be in charge. If a litter of puppies remained together beyond puppyhood, one of the pups would emerge as the strongest one, the one who calls the shots.

Once your puppy leaves the pack, he will look intuitively for a new leader. If he does not recognize you as that leader, he will try to assume that position for himself. Of course, it is hard to imagine your adorable SCWT puppy trying to be in charge when he is so small and seemingly helpless. You must remember that these are natural canine instincts. Do not cave in and allow your pup to get the upper "paw"!

Just as socialization is so important during these first 20 weeks, so too is your puppy's early education. He was born without any bad habits. He does not know what is good or bad behavior. If he does things like nipping and digging, it's because he is having fun and doesn't know that humans consider these things as "bad." It's your job to teach him proper puppy manners, and this is the best time to accomplish that…before he has developed bad habits, since it is much more difficult to "unlearn" or correct unacceptable learned behavior than to teach good behavior from the start.

THE CRITICAL SOCIALIZATION PERIOD

Canine research has shown that a puppy's 8th through 16th week is the most critical learning period of his life. This is when the puppy "learns to learn," a time when he needs positive experiences to build confidence and stability. Puppies who are not exposed to different people and situations outside the home during this period can grow up to be fearful and sometimes aggressive. This is also the best time for puppy lessons, since he has not yet acquired any bad habits that could undermine his ability to learn.

Make sure that all members of the family understand the importance of being consistent when training their new puppy. If you tell the puppy to stay off the sofa and your daughter allows him to cuddle on the couch to watch her favorite television show, your pup will be confused about what he is and is not allowed to do. Have a family conference before your pup comes home so that everyone understands the basic principles of puppy training and the rules you have set forth for the pup, and agrees to follow them.

The old adage that "an ounce of prevention is worth a pound of cure" is especially true when it comes to puppies. It is much easier to prevent inappropriate behavior than it is to change it. It's also easier and less stressful for the pup, since it will keep discipline to a minimum and create a more positive learning environment for him. That, in turn, will also be easier on you!

Here are a few commonsense tips to keep your belongings safe and your puppy out of trouble:

- Keep your closet doors closed and your shoes, socks and other apparel off the floor so your puppy can't get at them.
- Keep a secure lid on the trash container or put the trash where your puppy can't dig into it. He can't damage what he can't reach.
- Supervise your puppy at all times to make sure he is not getting into mischief. If he starts to chew the corner of the rug, you can distract him instantly by tossing a toy for him to fetch. You also will be able to whisk him outside when you notice that he is about to piddle on the carpet. If you can't see your puppy, you can't teach him or correct his behavior.

SOLVING PUPPY PROBLEMS

CHEWING AND NIPPING

Nipping at fingers and toes is normal puppy behavior. Chewing is also the way that puppies investigate their surroundings. However, you will have to teach your puppy that chewing anything other than his toys is not acceptable. That won't happen overnight, and at times puppy teeth will test your patience.

HAPPY PUPPIES COME RUNNING

Never call your puppy (or adult dog) to come to you and then scold him or discipline him when he gets there. He will make a natural association between coming to you and being scolded, and he will think he was a bad dog for coming to you. He will then be reluctant to come whenever he is called. Always praise your puppy every time he comes to you.

However, if you allow nipping and chewing to continue, just think about the damage that a mature SCWT can do with a full set of adult teeth.

Whenever your puppy nips your hand or fingers, cry out

A SMILE'S WORTH A MILE

Don't embark on your puppy's training course when you're not in the mood. Never train your puppy if you're feeling grouchy or impatient with him. Subjecting your puppy to your bad mood is a bad move. Your pup will sense your negative attitude, and neither of you will enjoy the session or have any measure of success. Always begin and end your training sessions on a happy note.

"Ouch!" in a loud voice, which should startle your puppy and stop him from nipping, even if only for a moment. Immediately distract him by offering a small treat or an appropriate toy for him to chew instead (which means having chew toys and puppy treats handy or in your pockets at all times). Praise him when he takes the toy and tell him what a good fellow he is. Praise is just as or even more important in puppy training as discipline and correction.

Puppies also tend to nip at children more often than adults, since they perceive little ones to be more vulnerable and more similar to their littermates. Teach your children appropriate responses to nipping behavior. If they are unable to handle it themselves, you may have to intervene. Puppy nips can be quite painful and a child's frightened reaction will only encourage a puppy to nip harder, which is a natural canine response. As with all other puppy situations, interaction between your SCWT puppy and children should be supervised.

Chewing on objects, not just family members' fingers and ankles, is also normal canine behavior that can be especially tedious (for the owner, not the pup) during the teething period when the puppy's adult teeth are coming in. At this stage, chewing just plain feels good. Furniture legs and cabinet corners are common puppy favorites. Shoes and other personal items also taste pretty good to a pup.

The best solution is, once again, prevention. If you value something, keep it tucked away and out of reach. You can't hide your dining-room table in a closet, but you can try to deflect the chewing by applying a bitter product made just to deter dogs from chewing. Available in a spray or cream, this substance is vile-tasting, although safe for dogs, and most puppies will avoid the forbidden object after one tiny taste. You also can apply the product to your leather leash if the puppy tries to chew on his lead during leash-training sessions.

Keep a ready supply of safe chews handy to offer your SCWT as a distraction when he starts to chew on something that's a "no-no." Remember, at this tender age he does not yet know what is permitted or forbidden, so you have to be "on call" every minute he's awake and on the prowl.

You may lose a treasure or two during puppy's growing-up period, and the furniture could sustain a nasty nick or two. These can be trying times, so be prepared for those inevitable accidents and comfort yourself in knowing that this too shall pass.

PUPPY WHINING

Puppies often cry and whine, just as infants and little children do. It's their way of telling us that they are lonely or in need of attention. Your puppy will miss his littermates and will feel insecure when he is left alone. You may be out of the house or just in another room, but he will still feel alone. During these times, the puppy's crate should be his personal comfort station, a place all his own where he can feel safe and secure. Once he learns that being alone is okay and not something to be feared, he will settle down without crying or objecting. You might want to leave a radio on while he is crated, as the sound of human voices can be soothing and will give the impression that people are around.

Give your puppy a favorite cuddly toy or chew toy to entertain him whenever he is crated. You will both be happier: the puppy because he is safe in his den and you because he is quiet, safe and not getting into puppy escapades that can wreak havoc in your house or cause him danger.

It's also important not to make a big fuss when he is released from the crate. That will make getting out of the crate more appealing than being in the crate, which is just the opposite of what you are trying to achieve.

The SCWT requires considerable exercise, grooming and attention. Do not purchase a Wheaten as an eye-catching home ornament!

EVERYDAY CARE OF YOUR

SOFT COATED
WHEATEN TERRIER

SPECIAL FEEDING CONSIDERATIONS

A SCWT should be fed sensibly on a high-quality diet, but protein content will vary according to whether or not the dog lives an especially active lifestyle; regardless, the breed is not usually fed high-protein foods. When selling a puppy, a carefully selected breeder should be able to give good advice in this regard, but it is generally accepted that dogs leading active lives need more protein than those spending most of their time by the fireside.

An owner should never be tempted to allow a dog to put on too much weight, for an overweight dog is more prone to health problems than one that is of correct weight for its size. Feeding any dog tidbits between meals will run the risk of causing the dog to be an unhealthy and over-weight dog in maturity. Soft Coated Wheaten Terriers are not generally difficult feeders, though, as with any breed of dog, there are always occasional exceptions. Some owners of SCWTs feed just

one meal each day, but others prefer to give two smaller portions; this is largely a matter of personal preference. Again, when buying a new puppy, it is sensible to seek the breeder's advice as to which he has found suits his dogs best in adulthood.

There are now numerous high-quality canine meals available, and one of them is sure to suit your SCWT. Because your SCWT's food has a bearing on coat, health and temperament, it is essential that the most suitable diet is selected for a SCWT of his age. It is fair to say, however, that even

Suitable food and water bowls should be provided for your SCWT. Clean water should always be available.

There is no better food for the SCWT puppy than its mother's milk. The puppies should be weaned to normal food by the time they are eight weeks of age.

experienced owners can be perplexed by the enormous range of foods available. Only understanding what is best for your dog will help you reach an informed decision. Once again, you should be able to obtain sound advice from your dog's breeder as to which food is considered most suitable. When you buy your puppy, the breeder should provide you with a diet sheet that gives details of exactly how your puppy has been fed. Of course, you will be at liberty to change that food, together with the frequency and timing of meals, as the youngster reaches adulthood, but this should be done gradually.

Some owners still prefer to feed fresh food, instead of one of the more convenient complete diets. However, there are so many of the latter now available, some scientifically balanced, that a lot will depend on personal preference. If you find the occasional "finicky eater," although you have to be very careful not to

FREE FEEDING

Many owners opt to feed their dogs by serving dry kibble in a feeder that is available to the dog all day. Arguably, this is the most convenient method of feeding an adult dog, but it may encourage the dog to become fussy about food or defensive over his bowl. Scheduled meals, with at least an hour before and after exercise, are healthiest for the dog's digestion.

unbalance an otherwise balanced diet, sometimes a little added fresh meat, or even gravy, will gain a dog's interest and stimulate the appetite.

If your dog suffers from an illness, a special diet may be prescribed. Depending on the actual illness, the diet selected by your veterinarian may be hypoallergenic, low in fat or low in protein. It could even be a combination of these. It is not certain that food allergies contribute to PLE and PLN in Soft Coated Wheaten Terriers, but it is suspected that this may be the case.

FEEDING THE PUPPY

Of course, your pup's very first food will be his dam's milk. There may be special situations in which pups fail to nurse, necessitating that the breeder hand-feed them with a formula, but for the most part pups spend the first weeks of life nursing from their dam. The breeder weans the pups by gradually introducing solid foods and decreasing the milk meals. Pups may even start themselves off on the weaning process, albeit inadvertently, if they snatch bites from their mom's food bowl.

By the time the pups are ready for new homes, they are fully weaned and eating a good puppy food. As a new owner, you may be thinking, "Great! The

Puppies should exhibit a hearty appetite during mealtimes. If your puppy is showing a lack of interest in his food, it could be your selection of food or possibly a more serious health problem. Consult your vet.

breeder has taken care of the hard part." Not so fast.

A puppy's first year of life is the time when all or most of his growth and development takes place. This is a delicate time, and diet plays a huge role in proper skeletal and muscular formation. Improper diet and exercise habits can lead to damaging problems that will compromise the dog's health and movement for his entire life. That being said, new owners should not worry needlessly. With the myriad types of food formulated specifically for growing pups of different-sized breeds, dog-food manufacturers have taken much of the guesswork out of feeding your puppy well. Since growth-food formulas are designed to provide the nutrition that a growing puppy needs, it is unnecessary and, in fact, can prove harmful to add supplements to the diet. Research has shown that too much of certain vitamin supplements and minerals predisposes a dog to skeletal problems. It's by no means a case of "if a

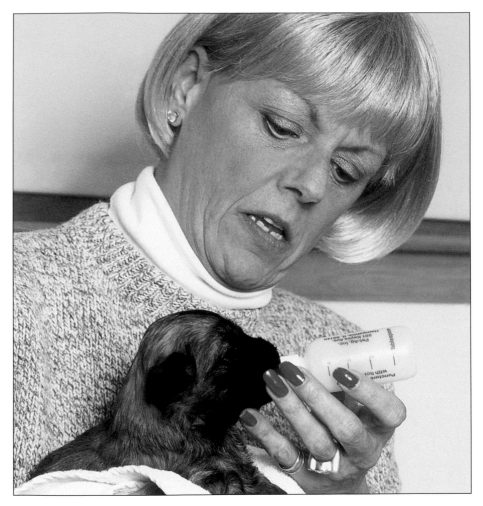

In situations where a puppy does not feed naturally from his mother, the puppy has to be hand-fed by the breeder.

little is good, a lot is better." At every stage of your dog's life, too much or too little in the way of nutrients can be harmful, which is why feeding a manufactured complete food is the easiest way to know that your dog is getting what he needs.

Because of a young pup's small body and accordingly small digestive system, his daily portion will be divided up into small meals throughout the day. This can mean starting off with three or more meals a day and decreasing the number of meals as the pup matures. Eventually you can feed only one meal a day, although it is generally thought that dividing the day's food into two meals on a morning/evening schedule is healthier for the dog's digestion.

Regarding the feeding schedule, feeding the pup at the same times and in the same place each day is important for both housebreaking purposes and establishing the dog's everyday routine. As for the amount to feed, growing puppies generally need proportionately more food per body weight than their adult counterparts, but a pup should never be allowed to gain excess weight. Dogs of all ages should be kept in proper body condition, but extra weight can strain a pup's developing frame, causing skeletal problems.

Watch your pup's weight as he grows and, if the recommended amounts seem to be too much or too little for your pup, consult the vet about appropriate dietary changes. Keep in mind that treats, although small, can quickly add up throughout the day, contributing unnecessary calories. Treats are fine when used prudently; opt for dog treats specially formulated to be healthy or for nutritious snacks like small pieces of cheese or cooked chicken.

FEEDING THE ADULT DOG

For the adult (meaning physically mature) dog, feeding properly is about maintenance, not growth. Again, correct weight is a concern. Your dog should appear fit and should have an evident "waist." His ribs should not be protruding (a sign of being underweight), but they should be covered by only a slight layer of fat. Under normal circumstances, an adult dog can be maintained fairly easily with a high-quality nutritionally complete adult-formula food.

Factor treats into your dog's overall daily caloric intake, and avoid offering table scraps. Overweight dogs are more prone to health problems. Research has even shown that obesity takes years off a dog's life. With that in mind, resist the urge to overfeed and over-treat. Don't make unnecessary additions to your dog's diet, whether with tidbits or with extra vitamins and minerals.

The amount of food needed for proper maintenance will vary depending on the individual dog's activity level, but you will be able to tell whether the daily portions are keeping him in good shape. With the wide variety of good

Breeders introduce their puppies to solid food slowly, alternating those feedings with sessions of nursing from the pups' mother.

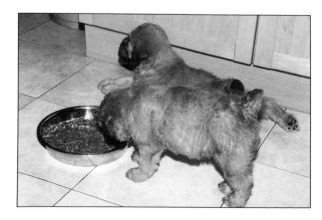

complete foods available, choosing what to feed is largely a matter of personal preference. Just as with the puppy, the adult dog should have consistency in his mealtimes and feeding place. In addition to a consistent routine, regular mealtimes also allow the owner to see how much his dog is eating. If the dog seems never to be satisfied or, likewise, becomes uninterested in his food, the owner will know right away that something is wrong and can consult the vet.

DIETS FOR THE AGING DOG

A good rule of thumb is that once a dog has reached 75% of his expected lifespan, he has reached "senior citizen" or geriatric status. Your SCWT will be considered a senior at about 9 or 10 years of age; based on his size, he has a projected lifespan of about 12 to 15 years.

What does aging have to do with your dog's diet? No, he won't get a discount at the local diner's early-bird special. Yes, he will require some dietary changes to accommodate the changes that come along with increased age. One change is that the older dog's dietary needs become more similar to those of a puppy. Specifically, dogs can metabolize more protein as youngsters and seniors than in the adult-mainte-nance stage. Discuss with your vet whether you need to switch to a

NOT HUNGRY?
No dog in his right mind would turn down his dinner, would he? If you notice that your dog has lost interest in his food, there could be any number of causes. Dental problems are a common cause of appetite loss, one that is often overlooked. If your dog has a toothache, a loose tooth or sore gums from infection, chances are it doesn't feel so good to chew. Think about when you've had a toothache! If your dog does not approach the food bowl with his usual enthusiasm, look inside his mouth for signs of a problem. Whatever the cause, you'll want to consult your vet so that your chow hound can get back to his happy, hungry self as soon as possible.

higher-protein or senior-formulated food or whether your current adult-dog food contains sufficient nutrition for the senior.

Watching the dog's weight remains essential, even more so in the senior stage. Older dogs are already more vulnerable to illness, and obesity only contributes to their susceptibility to problems. As the older dog becomes less active and thus exercises less, his regular portions may cause him to gain weight. At this point, you may consider decreasing his daily food intake or switching to a reduced-calorie food. As with other changes, you should consult your vet for advice.

DON'T FORGET THE WATER!

For a dog, it's always time for a drink! Regardless of what type of food he eats, there's no doubt that he needs plenty of water. Fresh cold water, in a clean bowl, should be freely available to your dog at all times. There are special circumstances, such as during puppy housebreaking, when you will want to monitor your pup's water intake so that you will be able to predict when he will need to relieve himself, but water must be available to him nonetheless. Water is essential for hydration and proper body function just as it is in humans.

You will get to know how much your dog typically drinks in a day. Of course, in the heat or if exercising vigorously, he will be more thirsty and will drink more. However, if he begins to drink noticeably more water for no apparent reason, this could signal any of various problems, and you are advised to consult your vet.

Water is the best drink for dogs. Some owners are tempted to give milk from time to time or to moisten dry food with milk, but dogs do not have the enzymes necessary to digest the lactose in milk, which is much different from the milk that nursing puppies receive. Therefore, stick with clean fresh water to quench your dog's thirst, and always have it readily available to him.

EXERCISE

SCWTs will readily accept as much exercise as their owners are prepared to give, but they are adaptable and don't seem to mind taking more leisurely days from time to time, such as during rainy weather. The Wheaten is an active breed, so exercise is important for both its health and happiness, as well as for maintaining muscular condition. However, exercise

SWITCHING FOODS

There are certain times in a dog's life when it becomes necessary to switch his food; for example, from puppy to adult food and then from adult to senior-dog food. Additionally, there may be "emergency" situations in which you can't find your dog's normal brand and have to offer something else temporarily. Some breeders caution that SCWTs do not handle dietary changes well; changes must only be done when truly needed. Anytime a change is made, for whatever reason, the switch must be done gradually. You don't want to upset the dog's stomach or end up with a dog who refuses to eat. A tried-and-true approach is, over the course of about a week, to mix a little of the new food in with the old, increasing the proportion of new to old as the days progress. At the end of the week, you'll be feeding his regular portions of the new food, and he will barely notice the change.

should be limited in young puppies, at least until the age of about six months.

How a SCWT is best exercised depends very much on the area in which one lives, notably whether in a country or city environment. However, if possible, a good brisk walk daily, with an opportunity for free run in a safe environment, should become routine in adulthood. Having said that, the SCWT again is very adaptable. While the dog will readily enjoy a good deal of exercise, he will also be content with a less active family, provided he is given the opportunity to play. Despite the fact that this is not one of the retrieving breeds, the SCWT will usually enjoy chasing things and, if games are introduced early in life, they will provide endless enjoyment throughout adulthood.

When allowing a dog to run free, safety is of utmost importance. For this reason, all possible escape routes should be thoroughly checked out before letting a dog off the lead. Of course, your yard also needs to be safely enclosed by fencing, which should be checked at regular intervals. For your SCWT's safety, do not feed him until one full hour has elapsed following vigorous exercise; likewise, allow him to relax for at least an hour following feeding before exercising.

Because this is a breed with a fairly long coat, the coat should

WEIGHT AND SEE!

When you look at yourself in the mirror each day, you get very used to what you see! It's only when you pull out last year's holiday outfit and can't zipper it that you notice that you've put on some pounds. Dog owners are the same way with their dogs. Often a few pounds go unnoticed, and it's not until some time passes or the vet remarks that your dog looks more than pleasantly plump that you realize what's happened. To avoid your pet's becoming obese right under your very nose, make a habit of routinely evaluating his condition with a hands-on test.

Can you feel, but not see, your dog's rib cage? Does your dog have a waist? His waist should be evident by touch and also visible from above and from the side. In top view, the dog's body should have an hourglass shape. These are indicators of good condition.

While it's not hard to spot an extremely skinny or overly rotund dog, it's the subtle changes that lead up to an under- or overweight condition of which we must be aware. If your dog's ribs are visible, he is too thin. Conversely, if you can't feel the ribs under too much fat, and if there's no indication of a waistline, your dog is overweight. Both of these conditions require changes to the diet. A trip or sometimes just a call to the vet will help you modify your dog's feeding.

always be checked thoroughly upon returning from outdoor activity and any debris that may have become entangled should be carefully removed.

Bear in mind that an overweight dog should never be suddenly over-exercised; instead he should be encouraged to increase exercise slowly. Not only is exercise essential to keep the dog's body fit, it is essential to his mental well-being. A bored dog will find something to do, which often manifests itself in some type of destructive behavior. In this sense, exercise is essential for the owner's mental well-being as well!

GROOMING

Upon selecting the Wheaten, you have taken upon yourself the responsibility of caring for his coat. The SCWT's coat requires considerable upkeep, even if you are just keeping him in a pet clip. From visiting a dog show or viewing photographs of show dogs, you can imagine how much upkeep is required to maintain that flowing, sculpted "terrier outline." Here we will outline what the pet owner needs to know to groom his Wheaten.

Whether grooming an adult or puppy, you must comb to the skin. You need to comb your Wheaten adult or puppy weekly, though the adolescent dog will need to be brushed daily. At around nine months of age, the adult coat

Letting your SCWT romp freely at his own pace in a safely enclosed yard is a good way to give him exercise.

begins to come through, a process that usually takes a few months to complete. Use a spray conditioner or a light water mist on the coat whenever brushing or combing.

Trimming a Wheaten properly requires experience, and you should not let your local groomer "have a go" if he does not know the breed. You do not want your Wheaten to look like a Poodle or a miniature Wolfhound!

Understandably, it takes practice to trim a Wheaten well, effectively shaping the coat to create the correct Wheaten image. Before attempting to trim your Wheaten, you must make sure that his coat is mat-free. Bathe the dog, using a dog shampoo and creme conditioner, and then blow dry the coat. You will need to use your grooming scissors and thinning shears plus your electric clipper (with blades #15, #10, #20 and #7), not to mention your slicker brush and comb. It's imperative that you use

SELECTING THE RIGHT BRUSHES AND COMBS

Will a rubber curry make my dog look slicker? Is a rake smaller than a pin brush? Do I choose nylon or natural bristles? Buying a dog brush can make the hairs on your head stand on end! Here's a quick once-over to educate you on the different types of brushes.

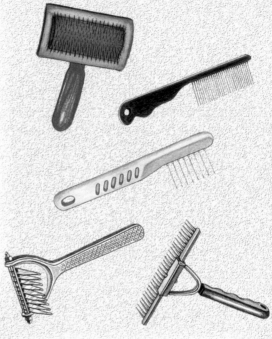

Slicker Brush: Fine metal prongs closely set on a curved base. Used to remove dead coat from the undercoat of medium- to long-coated breeds.

Pin Brush: Metal pins, often covered with rubber tips, set on an oval base. Used to remove shedding hair and is gentler than a slicker brush.

Metal Comb: Steel teeth attached to a steel handle; the closeness and size of the teeth vary greatly. A "flea comb" has tiny teeth set very closely together and is used to find fleas in a dog's coat. Combs with wider teeth are used for detangling longer coats.

Rake: Long-toothed comb with a short handle. Used to remove undercoat from heavily coated breeds with dense undercoats.

Soft-bristle Brush: Nylon or natural bristles set in a plastic or wood base. Used on short coats or long coats (without undercoats).

Rubber Curry: Rubber prongs, with or without a handle. Used for short-coated dogs. Good for use during shampooing.

Combination Brushes: Two-sided brush with a different type of bristle on each side; for example, pin brush on one side and slicker on the other, or bristle brush on one side and pin brush on the other. An economical choice if you need two kinds of brushes.

Grooming Glove: Sometimes called a hound glove; used to give sleek-coated dogs a once-over.

sharp blades, as the Wheaten's soft coat can be harmed by dull blades.

Using the scissors, trim the head, tail and legs first. Do not overtrim the fall over the eyes or the leg furnishings if you have any intention of showing. The dog's muzzle should always be adorned with long, flowing hair, and the fore and hind leg furnishings should be no shorter than 2.5 inches. Pet owners often like to see their Wheaten's lovely eyes and therefore trim the fall. Starting from the front of the ear to the center of the eye, trim the hair on the side of the face with the thinning shears. You want to leave the hair on the top of the head long, trimming in a straight line from the top of the skull to the muzzle,

leave the hair on the cheeks short. The hair on the top of the head is scissored fairly short between the ears, well blended into the coat.

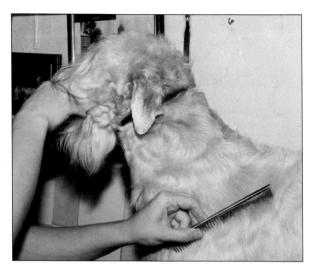

The clipper is used to trim the ears (#10 on the inside and #7 on the outside), working from the center of the ear to the outside. Do not overtrim the ears to expose the leather. Leave a nice cottony fuzz on the ears. The fringe should be removed with your scissors. The neck is trimmed close. Be careful not to shave the beard, which should begin at about the center of the eye and hang down a few inches past the chin. Only in cases of an extremely thick beard should you have to trim it at all

A steel comb is used to keep the Wheaten's coat neat and tangle-free.

The neck is one of the places where the coat is trimmed, using thinning shears.

When using an electric clipper, experience and care are required. Clippers are used more regularly by American groomers; more British fanciers opt to use the thinning shears.

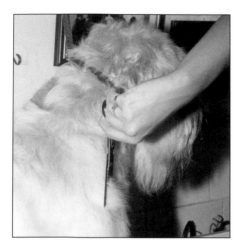

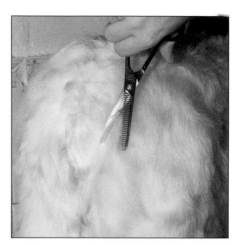

LEFT: The show dog is shaped all over the body to create the proper outline. RIGHT: The tail will require some tidying up as well.

(to avoid that nanny goat look that doesn't say "Wheaten"). Some practice is required with your scissors or thinning shears to blend the coat on the back of the neck into the coat on the head and the shorter throat hair into the longer neck hair.

You want to clip the neck and chest area coming toward the legs, as well as the area above the rear legs, usually about one-quarter inch. The topline (from the back of the head, down the neck and

The excess hair on the bottom of the foot should be trimmed carefully with flat scissors.

back) should be trimmed straight, approximately three-quarters an inch in length. You want to clip from the front to the rear with the lie of the coat. The underside can be trimmed with the #20 blade, to give the dog the desired tuck-up between the hind legs. Be careful around the dog's penis or vulva. You can trim a little shorter around these to prevent the dog from urinating on him/herself. In the warm months, you may want to use a #10 blade on the belly to provide some ventilation down there. Hair around the rib cage should extend about 2 inches below the dog's trunk.

The legs are an important part of the trimming process. Using your scissors and your slicker brush, trim the front legs to appear cylindrical and the rear legs to balance and follow the bend. Using a curved shear, trim around the feet closely. The coat on the underside of the foot should be trimmed shorter. The #15 blade is handy to clean out the coat between the foot pads. Do not remove the hair between the toes. Don't forget the tail, which should be scissored to the shape of a small cone.

The breed standard requires the ears to be "relieved of fringe, but not taken down to the leather." Therefore, the ear fringing is trimmed to set off the "V" shape of the ear, bearing in mind that if too much fringing is left on, it can weigh down the ear and make it look uncharacteristic.

Although many pet Wheatens are not trimmed, they must have attention given to their coats at least on a weekly basis. All owners will find that, because this breed does not shed its coat, instead the coat will mat. If any mats are allowed to build up, they should be carefully removed as soon as they are spotted! It helps if the coat is moistened when removing a mat. Always work from the skin outward, otherwise the knot will simply tighten. It is also important that any little pieces of twigs and other debris that have become entrapped in the coat are removed immediately following time spent outdoors.

BATHING

In general, dogs need to be bathed only a few times a year, possibly

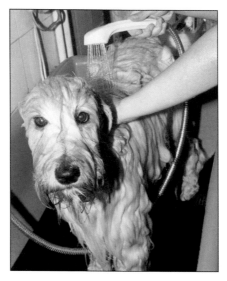

After a thorough brushing, the dog should be wet down.

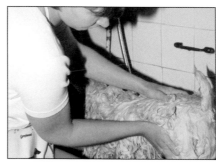

Shampoo made especially for dogs should be applied section by section.

During drying, the dog should be brushed through or the coat will dry in tangles.

The grooming and bathing of a Wheaten are time-consuming but necessary tasks. Owners must devote the time to their dogs or be willing to pay a professional groomer to handle the job.

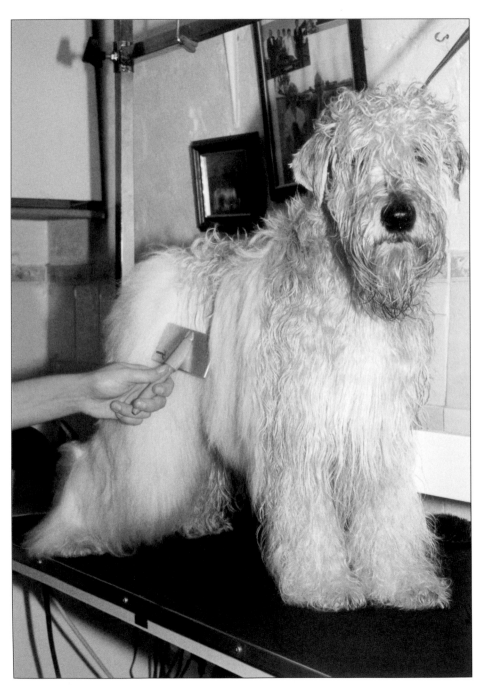

more often if your dog gets into something messy or if he starts to smell like a dog. Show Wheatens are bathed one to three days before a show, depending on the coat quality. Wheatens can be bathed on a regular basis with no ill effects to their coats.

If you give your dog his first bath when he is young, he will become accustomed to the process. Wrestling a dog into the tub or chasing a freshly shampooed dog who has escaped from the bath will be no fun! Most dogs don't naturally enjoy their baths, but you at least want yours to cooperate with you.

Before bathing the dog, have the items you'll need close at hand. First, decide where you will bathe the dog. You should have a tub or basin with a non-slip surface. Small dogs can even be bathed in a sink. In warm weather, some like to use a portable pool in the yard, although you'll want to make sure your dog doesn't head for the nearest dirt pile following his bath. You will also need a hose or shower spray to wet the coat thoroughly, a shampoo formulated for dogs, absorbent towels and perhaps a blow dryer. Human shampoos are too harsh for dogs' coats and will dry them out.

Before wetting the dog, give him a brush-through to remove any dead hair, dirt and mats. Make sure he is at ease in the tub

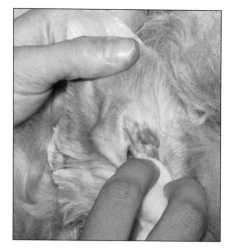

The ears should be cleaned with a cotton ball and ear powder, available from your local pet shop. Report any odors or evidence of parasites to your vet.

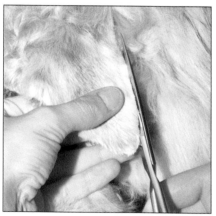

The fringe on the ears should be trimmed to accentuate the "V" shape.

and have the water at a comfortable temperature. Begin bathing by wetting the coat all the way down to the skin. Massage in the shampoo, keeping it away from his face and eyes. Rinse him thoroughly, again avoiding the eyes and ears, as you don't want to get water into the ear canals. A thorough rinsing is important, as shampoo residue is drying and itchy to the dog. After rinsing,

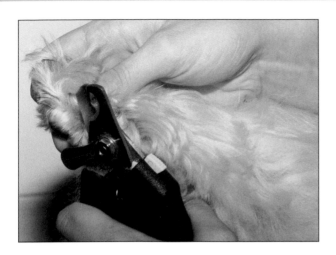

your individual dog. Look at his nails from time to time and clip as needed; a good way to know when it's time for a trim is if you hear your dog clicking as he walks across the floor.

There are several types of nail clippers and even electric nail-

The earlier your Wheaten is introduced to the nail-clipping procedure, the easier it will go for both of you.

wrap him in a towel to absorb the initial moisture. You can finish drying with either a towel or a blow dryer on low heat, held at a safe distance from the dog. You should keep the dog indoors and away from drafts until he is completely dry.

NAIL CLIPPING

Having his nails trimmed is not on many dogs' lists of favorite things to do. With this in mind, you will need to accustom your puppy to the procedure at a young age so that he will sit still (well, as still as he can) for his pedicures. Long nails can cause the dog's feet to spread, which is not good for him; likewise, long nails can hurt if they unintention-ally scratch, not good for you!

Some dogs' nails are worn down naturally by regular walking on hard surfaces, so the frequency with which you clip depends on

THE MONTHLY GRIND

If your dog doesn't like the feeling of nail clippers or if you're not comfortable using them, you may wish to try an electric nail grinder. This tool has a small sandpaper disc on the end that rotates to grind the nails down. Some feel that using a grinder reduces the risk of cutting into the quick; this can be true if the tool is used properly. Usually you will be able to tell where the quick is before you get to it. A benefit of the grinder is that it creates a smooth finish on the nails so that there are no ragged edges.

Because the tool makes noise, your dog should be introduced to it before the actual grinding takes place. Turn it on and let your dog hear the noise; turn it off and let him inspect it with you holding it. Use the grinder gently, holding it firmly and progressing a little at a time until you reach the proper length. Look at the nail as you grind so that you do not go too short. Stop at any indication that you are nearing the quick. It will take a few sessions for both you and the puppy to get used to the grinder. Make sure that you don't let his hair get tangled in the grinder!

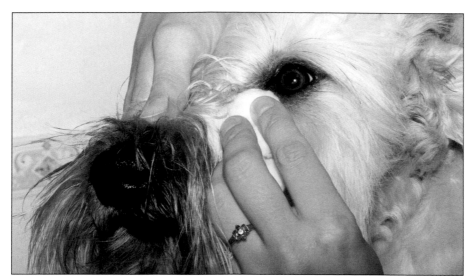

Carefully inspect your Wheaten's eyes. They should be clear, without any debris or signs of cloudiness. Tear stains are easily removed with products available from your local pet shop.

grinding tools made for dogs; first we'll discuss using the clipper. To start, have your clipper ready and some doggie treats on hand. You want your pup to view his nail-clipping sessions in a positive light, and what better way to convince him than with food? You may want to enlist the help of an assistant to comfort the pup and offer treats as you concentrate on the clipping itself. The guillotine-type clipper is thought of by many as the easiest type to use; the nail tip is inserted into the opening, and blades on the top and bottom snip it off in one clip.

Start by grasping the pup's paw; a little pressure on the foot pad causes the nail to extend, making it easier to clip. Clip off a little at a time. If you can see the "quick," which is a blood vessel that runs through each nail, you will know how much to trim, as you do not want to cut into the quick. On that note, if you do cut the quick, which will cause bleeding, you can stem the flow of blood with a styptic pencil or other clotting agent. If you mistakenly nip the quick, do not panic or fuss, as this will cause the pup to be afraid. Simply reassure the pup, stop the bleeding and move on to the next nail. Don't be discouraged; you will become a professional canine pedicurist with practice.

You may or may not be able to see the quick, so it's best to just clip off a small bit at a time. If you see a dark dot in the center of the nail, this is the quick and your cue to stop clipping. Tell the puppy he's a "good boy" and offer a piece of treat with each nail. You can also use nail-clipping time to examine the footpads, making sure that they are not dry and cracked and that nothing has become embedded in them.

The nail grinder, the second choice, is many owners' first choice. Accustoming the puppy to the sound of the grinder and sensation of the buzz presents fewer challenges than the clipper, and there's no chance of cutting through the quick. Use the grinder on a low setting and always talk soothingly to your dog. He won't mind his salon visit, and he'll have nicely polished nails as well.

EAR CLEANING

While keeping your dog's ears clean unfortunately will not cause him to "hear" your commands any better, it will protect him from ear infection and ear-mite infestation. In addition, a dog's ears are vulnerable to waxy build-up and to collecting foreign matter from the outdoors. Look in your dog's ears regularly to ensure that they look pink, clean and otherwise healthy. Even if they look fine, an odor in the ears signals a problem and means it's time to call the vet.

A dog's ears should be cleaned regularly; once a week is suggested, and you can do this along with your regular brushing. Using a cotton ball or pad and, never probing into the ear canal, wipe the ear gently. You can use an ear-cleansing liquid or powder available from your vet or pet-supply store; alternatively, you might prefer to use home-made solutions with ingredients like one part white vinegar and one part hydrogen peroxide. Ask your vet about home remedies before you attempt to concoct something on your own!

Keep your dog's ears free of excess hair by plucking it as needed. If done gently, this will be painless for the dog. Look for wax, brown droppings (a sign of ear mites), redness or any other abnormalities. At the first sign of a problem, contact your vet so that he can prescribe an appropriate medication.

IDENTIFICATION AND TRAVEL

ID FOR YOUR DOG

You love your SCWT and want to keep him safe. Of course you take every precaution to prevent his escaping from the yard or becoming lost or stolen. You have a sturdy high fence and you

A COAT IN THE SUMMER

A dog's long or heavy coat is designed for insulation in any type of weather, so think again before giving your dog a summer haircut. Shaving down his coat in warm weather will affect his body's natural temperature regulation and is neither necessary nor beneficial.

always keep your dog on lead when out and about in public places. If your dog is not properly identified, however, you are overlooking a major aspect of his safety. We hope to never be in a situation where our dog is missing, but we should practice prevention in the unfortunate case that this happens; identification greatly increases the chances of your dog's being returned to you.

There are several ways to identify your dog. First, the traditional dog tag should be a staple in your dog's wardrobe, attached to his everyday collar. Tags can be made of sturdy plastic and various metals and should include your contact information so that a person who finds the dog can get in touch with you right away to arrange his return. Many people today enjoy the wide range of decorative tags available, so have fun and create a tag to match your dog's personality. Of course, it is important that the tag stays on the collar, so have a secure "O" ring attachment; you also can explore the type of tag that slides right onto the collar.

In addition to the ID tag, which every dog should wear even if identified by another method, two other forms of identification have become popular: microchipping and tattooing. In microchipping, a tiny scannable chip is painlessly inserted under the dog's skin. The number is

registered to you so that, if your lost dog turns up at a clinic or shelter, the chip can be scanned to retrieve your contact information.

The advantage of the microchip is that it is a permanent form of ID, but there are some factors to consider. Several different companies make microchips, and not all are compatible with the others' scanning devices. It's best to find a company with a universal microchip that can be read by scanners made by other companies as well. It won't do any good to have the dog chipped if the information cannot be retrieved. Also, not every humane society, shelter and clinic is equipped with a scanner, although more and more facilities are equipping themselves. In fact,

Multi-Wheaten families are wise to select a station wagon for travel. You will need a vehicle large enough to accommodate two dog crates.

The safest way to travel with your dogs is in their crates, although the dogs might have a different idea!

many shelters microchip dogs that they adopt out to new homes.

In the US, there are five or six major microchip manufacturers as well as a few databases. The American Kennel Club's Companion Animal Recovery unit works in conjunction with HomeAgain™ Companion Animal Retrieval System (Schering-Plough). In the UK, The Kennel Club is affiliated with the National Pet Register, operated by Wood Green Animal Shelters.

Because the microchip is not visible to the eye, the dog must wear a tag that states that he is microchipped so that whoever picks him up will know to have him scanned. He of course also should have a tag with contact information in case his chip cannot be read. Humane societies and veterinary clinics offer microchipping service, which is usually very affordable.

Though less popular than microchipping, tattooing is another permanent method of ID for dogs. Most vets perform this service, and there are also clinics that perform dog tattooing. This is also an affordable procedure and one that will not cause much discomfort for the dog. It is best to put the tattoo in a visible area, such as the ear, to deter theft. It is sad to say that there are cases of dogs' being stolen and sold to research laboratories, but such laboratories will not accept tattooed dogs.

To ensure that the tattoo is effective in aiding your dog's return to you, the tattoo number must be registered with a national organization. That way, when someone finds a tattooed dog, a phone call to the registry will

CAR CAUTION

You may like to bring your canine companion along on the daily errands, but if you will be running in and out from place to place and can't bring him indoors with you, leave him at home. Your dog should never be left alone in the car, not even for a minute...never! A car heats up very quickly, and even a cracked-open window will not help. In fact, leaving the window cracked will be dangerous if the dog becomes uncomfortable and tries to escape. When in doubt, leave your dog home, where you know he will be safe.

quickly match the dog with his owner.

HIT THE ROAD

Car travel with your SCWT may be limited to necessity only, such as trips to the vet, or you may bring your dog along almost everywhere you go. This will depend much on your individual dog and how he reacts to rides in the car. You can begin desensitizing your dog to car travel as a pup so that it's something that he's used to. Still, some dogs suffer from motion sickness. Your vet may prescribe a medication for this if trips in the car pose a problem for your dog. At the very least, you will need to get him to the vet, so he will need to tolerate these trips with the least amount of hassle possible.

Start taking your pup on short trips, maybe just around the block to start. If he is fine with short trips, lengthen your rides a little at a time. Start to take him on your errands or just for drives around town. By this time, it will be easy to tell whether your dog is a born traveler or would prefer staying at home when you are on the road.

Of course, safety is a concern for dogs in the car. First, he must travel securely, not left loose to roam about the car where he could be injured or distract the driver. A young pup can be held by a passenger initially but should soon graduate to a travel crate,

DOGGONE!

Wendy Ballard is the editor and publisher of the *DogGone*™ newsletter, which comes out bi-monthly and features fun articles by dog owners who love to travel with their dogs. The newsletter includes information about fun places to go with your dogs, including popular vacation spots, dog-friendly hotels, parks, campgrounds, resorts, etc., as well as interesting activities to do with your dog, such as flyball, agility and much more. You can subscribe to the publication by contacting the publisher at PO Box 651155, Vero Beach, FL 32965-1155.

which can be the same crate he uses in the home. Other options include a car harness (like a seat belt for dogs) and partitioning the back of the car with a gate made for this purpose.

Bring along what you will need for the dog. He should wear his collar and ID tags, of course, and you should bring his leash, water (and food if a long trip) and clean-up materials for potty breaks and in case of motion sickness. Always keep your dog on his leash when you make stops, and never leave him alone in the car. Many a dog has died from the heat inside a closed car; this does not take much time at all. A dog left alone inside a car can also be a target for thieves.

Your SCWT looks to you for its education. Whether you are training for the show ring or simply for a life as a companion, your dog needs regular attention and instruction.

SOFT COATED WHEATEN TERRIER

BASIC TRAINING PRINCIPLES: PUPPY VS. ADULT

There's a big difference between training an adult dog and training a young puppy. With a young puppy, everything is new! At eight to ten weeks of age, he will be experiencing many things, and he has nothing with which to compare these experiences. Up to this point, he has been with his dam and littermates, not one-on-one with people except in his interactions with his breeder and visitors to the litter.

When you first bring the puppy home, he is eager to please you. This means that he accepts doing things your way. During the next couple of months, he will absorb the basis of everything he needs to know for the rest of his life. This early age is even referred to as the "sponge" stage. After that, for the next 18 months, it's up to you to reinforce good manners by building on the foundation that you've established. Once your puppy is reliable in basic commands and behavior and has reached the

A Wheaten puppy is a dry sponge waiting to soak up all the education and training it possibly can.

appropriate age, you may gradually introduce him to some of the interesting sports, games and activities available to pet owners and their dogs.

Raising your puppy is a family affair. Each member of the family must know what rules to set forth for the puppy and how to use the same one-word commands to mean exactly the same thing every time. Even if yours is a large family, one person will soon be considered by the pup to be the leader, the Alpha person in his pack, the "boss" who must be obeyed. Often that highly regarded person turns out to be the one who feeds the puppy. Food ranks very high on the puppy's list of important things! That's why your puppy is rewarded with small treats along with verbal praise when he responds to you correctly. As the puppy learns to do what you want him to do, the food rewards are gradually eliminated and only the praise remains. If you were to keep up with the food treats, you could have two problems on your hands—an obese dog and a beggar.

Training begins the minute your SCWT puppy steps through the doorway of your home, so don't make the mistake of putting the puppy on the floor and telling him by your actions to "Go for it! Run wild!" Even if this is your first puppy, you must act as if you know what you're doing: be the boss. An uncertain pup may be terrified to move, while a bold one will be ready to take you at your word and start plotting to destroy the house. Before you collected your puppy, you decided where his own special place would be, and that's where to put him when you first arrive home. Give him a house tour after he has investigated his area and had a nap and a bathroom "pit stop."

It's worth mentioning here that, if you've adopted an adult dog that is completely trained to your liking, lucky you! You're off the hook! However, if that dog

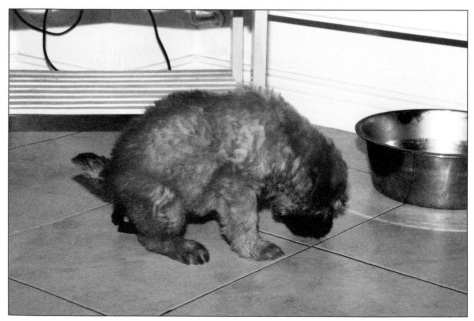

Like human babies, puppies cannot control their excretory functions. They need to be trained where and when to relieve themselves. It requires patience and understanding from the new owner.

spent his life up to this point in a kennel, or even in a good home but without any real training, be prepared to tackle the job ahead. A dog three years of age or older with no previous training cannot be blamed for not knowing what he was never taught. While the dog is trying to understand and learn your rules, at the same time he has to unlearn many of his previously self-taught habits and general view of the world.

Working with a professional trainer will speed up your progress with an adopted adult dog. You'll need patience, too. Some new rules may be close to impossible for the dog to accept. After all, he's been successful so far by doing everything his way! (Patience again.) He may agree with your instruction for a few days and then slip back into his old ways, so you must be just as consistent and understanding in your teaching as you would be with a puppy. (More patience needed yet again!) Your dog has to learn to pay attention to your voice, your family, the daily routine, new smells, new sounds and, in some cases, even a new climate.

One of the most important things to find out about a newly adopted adult dog is his reaction to children (yours and others), strangers and your friends, and how he acts upon meeting other dogs. If he was not socialized with dogs as a puppy, this could be a major problem. This does not mean that he's a "bad" dog, a vicious dog or an aggressive dog; rather, it means that he has no idea how to read another dog's body language. There's no way for him to tell whether the other dog is a friend or foe. Survival instinct takes over, telling him to attack first and ask questions later. This definitely calls for professional help and, even then, may not be a behavior that can be corrected 100% reliably (or even at all). If you have a puppy, this is why it is so very important to introduce your young puppy properly to other puppies and "dog-friendly" adult dogs.

CREATURES OF HABIT

Canine behaviorists and trainers aptly describe dogs as "creatures of habit," meaning that dogs respond to structure in their daily lives and welcome a routine. Do not interpret this to mean that dogs enjoy endless repetition in their training sessions. Dogs get bored just as humans do. Keep training sessions interesting and exciting. Vary the commands and the locations in which you practice. Give short breaks for play in between lessons. A bored student will never be the best performer in the class.

HOUSE-TRAINING YOUR SCWT
Dogs are tactility-oriented when it comes to house-training. In other words, they respond to the surface on which they are given approval to eliminate. The choice is yours (the dog's version is in parentheses): The lawn (including the neighbors' lawns)? A bare patch of earth under a tree (where people like to sit and relax in the summertime)? Concrete steps or patio (all sidewalks, garage and basement floors)? The curbside (watch out for cars)? A small area of crushed stone in a corner of the yard (mine!)? The latter is the best choice if you can manage it, because it will remain strictly for the dog's use and is easy to keep clean.

You can start out with paper-training indoors and switch over to an outdoor surface as the puppy matures and gains control over his need to eliminate. For the nay-sayers, don't worry—this won't mean that the dog will soil on every piece of newspaper lying around the house. You are training him to go outside, remember? Starting out by paper-training often is the only choice for a city dog.

WHEN YOUR PUPPY'S "GOT TO GO"
Your puppy's need to relieve himself is seemingly non-stop, but signs of improvement will be seen each week. From 8 to 10 weeks old, the puppy will have to be taken outside every time he wakes up, about 10-15 minutes after every meal and after every period of play—all day long, from first thing in the morning until his bedtime! That's a total of ten or more trips per day to teach the puppy where it's okay to relieve himself. With that schedule in mind, you can see that house-

DAILY SCHEDULE
How many relief trips does your puppy need per day? A puppy up to the age of 14 weeks will need to go outside about 8 to 12 times per day! You will have to take the pup out any time he starts sniffing around the floor or turning in small circles, as well as after naps, meals, games and lessons or whenever he's released from his crate. Once the puppy is 14 to 22 weeks of age, he will require only 6 to 8 relief trips. At the ages of 22 to 32 weeks, the puppy will require about 5 to 7 trips. Adult dogs typically require 4 relief trips per day, in the morning, afternoon, evening and late at night.

TIDY BOY

Clean by nature, dogs do not like to soil their dens, which in effect are their crates or sleeping quarters. Unless not feeling well, dogs will not defecate or urinate in their crates. Crate training capitalizes on the dog's natural desire to keep his den clean. Be conscientious about giving the puppy as many opportunities to relieve himself outdoors as possible. Reward the puppy for correct behavior. Praise him and pat him whenever he "goes" in the correct location. Even the tidiest of puppies can have potty accidents, so be patient and dedicate more energy to helping your puppy achieve a clean lifestyle.

training a young puppy is not a part-time job. It requires someone to be home all day.

If that seems overwhelming or impossible, do a little planning. For example, plan to pick up your puppy at the start of a vacation period. If you can't get home in the middle of the day, plan to hire a dog-sitter or ask a neighbor to come over to take the pup outside, feed him his lunch and then take him out again about ten or so minutes after he's eaten. Also make arrangements with that person or another to be your "emergency" contact if you have to stay late on the job. Remind yourself—repeatedly—that this

hectic schedule improves as the puppy gets older.

HOME WITHIN A HOME

Your SCWT puppy needs to be confined to one secure, puppy-proof area when no one is able to watch his every move. Generally the kitchen is the place of choice because the floor is washable. Likewise, it's a busy family area that will accustom the pup to a variety of noises, everything from pots and pans to the telephone, blender and dishwasher. He will also be enchanted by the smell of your cooking (and will never be critical when you burn something). An exercise pen (also called an "ex-pen," a puppy version of a playpen) within the room of choice is an excellent means of confinement for a young pup. He can see out and has a certain amount of space in which to run about, but he is safe from dangerous things like electrical

A dog trained to relieve itself on grass will always seek this surface for the purpose of relieving itself.

cords, heating units, trash baskets or open kitchen-supply cabinets. Place the pen where the puppy will not get a blast of heat or air conditioning.

EXTRA! EXTRA!

The headlines read: "Puppy Piddles Here!" Breeders commonly use newspapers to line their whelping pens, so puppies learn to associate newspapers with relieving themselves. Do not use newspapers to line your pup's crate, as this will signal to your puppy that it is OK to urinate in his crate. If you choose to paper-train your puppy, you will layer newspapers on a section of the floor near the door he uses to go outside. You should encourage the puppy to use the papers to relieve himself, and bring him there whenever you see him getting ready to go. Little by little, you will reduce the size of the newspaper-covered area so that the puppy will learn to relieve himself "on the other side of the door."

In the pen, you can put a few toys, his bed (which can be his crate if the dimensions of pen and crate are compatible) and a few layers of newspaper in one small corner, just in case. A water bowl can be hung at a convenient height on the side of the ex-pen so it won't become a splashing pool for an innovative puppy. His food dish can go on the floor, near but not under the water bowl.

Crates are something that pet owners are at last getting used to for their dogs. Wild or domestic canines have always preferred to sleep in den-like safe spots, and that is exactly what the crate provides. How often have you seen adult dogs that choose to sleep under a table or chair even though they have full run of the house? It's the den connection.

In your "happy" voice, use the word "Crate" every time you put the pup into his den. If he's new to a crate, toss in a small biscuit for him to chase the first few times. At night, after he's been outside, he should sleep in his crate. The crate may be kept in his designated area at night or, if you want to be sure to hear those wake-up yips in the morning, put the crate in a corner of your bedroom. However, don't make any response whatsoever to whining or crying. If he's completely ignored, he'll settle down and get to sleep.

CANINE DEVELOPMENT SCHEDULE

It is important to understand how and at what age a puppy develops into adulthood. If you are a puppy owner, consult the following Canine Development Schedule to determine the stage of development your puppy is currently experiencing. This knowledge will help you as you work with the puppy in the weeks and months ahead.

PERIOD	AGE	CHARACTERISTICS
FIRST TO THIRD	BIRTH TO SEVEN WEEKS	Puppy needs food, sleep and warmth and responds to simple and gentle touching. Needs mother for security and disciplining. Needs littermates for learning and interacting with other dogs. Pup learns to function within a pack and learns pack order of dominance. Begin socializing pup with adults and children for short periods. Pup begins to become aware of his environment.
FOURTH	EIGHT TO TWELVE WEEKS	Brain is fully developed. Pup needs socializing with outside world. Remove from mother and littermates. Needs to change from canine pack to human pack. Human dominance necessary. Fear period occurs between 8 and 12 weeks. Avoid fright and pain.
FIFTH	THIRTEEN TO SIXTEEN WEEKS	Training and formal obedience should begin. Less association with other dogs, more with people, places, situations. Period will pass easily if you remember this is pup's change-to-adolescence time. Be firm and fair. Flight instinct prominent. Permissiveness and over-disciplining can do permanent damage. Praise for good behavior.
JUVENILE	FOUR TO EIGHT MONTHS	Another fear period about 7 to 8 months of age. It passes quickly, but be cautious of fright and pain. Sexual maturity reached. Dominant traits established. Dog should understand sit, down, come and stay by now.

NOTE: THESE ARE APPROXIMATE TIME FRAMES. ALLOW FOR INDIVIDUAL DIFFERENCES IN PUPPIES.

Good bedding for a young puppy is an old folded bath towel or an old blanket, something that is easily washable and disposable if necessary ("accidents" will happen!). Never put newspaper in the puppy's crate. Also, those old ideas about adding a clock to replace his mother's heartbeat, or a hot-water bottle to replace her warmth, are just that—old ideas. The clock could drive the puppy nuts, and the hot-water bottle could end up as a very soggy waterbed. An extremely good breeder would have introduced your puppy to the crate by letting two pups sleep together for a couple of nights, followed by several nights alone. How thankful you will be if you found that breeder!

Safe toys in the pup's crate or area will keep him occupied, but monitor their condition closely. Discard any toys that show signs

Your SCWT will grow up to accept his crate as his "second home." Naturally he will make every effort to keep his sleeping area clean; using the crate as a den makes perfect sense to the dog.

POTTY COMMAND

Most dogs love to please their masters; there are no bounds to what dogs will do to make their owners happy. The potty command is a good example of this theory. If toileting on command makes the master happy, then more power to him. Puppies will obligingly piddle if it really makes their keepers smile. Some owners can be creative about which word they will use to command their dogs to relieve themselves. Some popular choices are "Potty," "Tinkle," "Piddle," "Let's go," "Hurry up" and "Toilet." Give the command every time your puppy goes into position and the puppy will begin to associate his business with the command.

of being chewed to bits. Squeaky parts, bits of stuffing or plastic or any other small pieces can cause intestinal blockage or possibly choking if swallowed.

PROGRESSING WITH POTTY-TRAINING
After you've taken your puppy out and he has relieved himself in the area you've selected, he can have some free time with the family as long as there is someone responsible for watching him. That doesn't mean just someone in the same room who is watching TV or busy on the computer, but one person who is doing nothing other than keeping an eye on the pup,

playing with him on the floor and helping him understand his position in the pack.

This first taste of freedom will let you begin to set the house rules. If you don't want the dog on the furniture, now is the time to prevent his first attempts to jump up onto the couch. The word to use in this case is "Off," not "Down." "Down" is the word you will use to teach the down position, which is something entirely different.

Most corrections at this stage come in the form of simply distracting the puppy. Instead of telling him "No" for "Don't chew the carpet," distract the chomping puppy with a toy and he'll forget about the carpet.

As you are playing with the pup, do not forget to watch him closely and pay attention to his body language. Whenever you see him begin to circle or sniff, take the puppy outside to relieve himself. If you are paper-training, put him back into his confined area on the newspapers. In either case, praise him as he eliminates while he actually is in the act of relieving himself. Three seconds after he has finished is too late. You'll be praising him for running toward you or picking up a toy or whatever he may be doing at that moment, and that's not what you want to be praising him for. Timing is a vital tool in all dog training. Use it!

Remove soiled newspapers immediately and replace them with clean ones. You may want to take a small piece of soiled paper and place it in the middle of the new clean papers, as the scent will attract him to that spot when it's time to go again. That scent attraction is why it's so important to clean up any messes made in the house by using a product specially made to eliminate the odor of dog urine and droppings. Regular household cleansers won't do the trick. Pet shops sell the best pet deodorizers. Invest in the largest container you can find.

Scent attraction eventually will lead your pup to his chosen spot outdoors; this is the basis of outdoor training. When you take your puppy outside to relieve himself, use a one-word command such as "Outside" or "Go-potty" (that's one word to the puppy!) as you pick him up and attach his leash. Then put him down in his

Limit the amount of water you offer your growing Wheaten puppy. Offer him water during the day when he's playing, but remove the water by early evening until house-training is completely accomplished.

What goes in must come out! Potty training is the art of managing your puppy's input and output.

area. If for any reason you can't carry him, snap the leash on quickly and lead him to his spot. Now comes the hard part—hard for you, that is. Just stand there until he urinates and defecates. Move him a few feet in one direction or another if he's just sitting there looking at you, but remember that this is neither playtime nor time for a walk. This is strictly a business trip! Then, as he circles and squats (remember your timing!), give him a quiet "Good dog" as praise. If you start to jump for joy, ecstatic over his performance, he'll do one of two things: he will either stop mid-stream, as it were, or he'll do it again for you—in the house—and expect you to be just as delighted!

Give him five minutes or so and, if he doesn't go in that time, take him back indoors to his confined area and try again in another ten minutes, or immedi-

ately if you see him sniffing and circling. By careful observation, you'll soon work out a successful schedule.

Accidents, by the way, are just that—accidents. Clean them up quickly and thoroughly, without comment, after the puppy has been taken outside to finish his business and then put back into his area or crate. If you witness an accident in progress, say "No!" in a stern voice and get the pup outdoors immediately. No punishment is needed. You and your puppy are just learning each other's language, and sometimes it's easy to miss a puppy's message. Chalk it up to experience and watch more closely from now on.

KEEPING THE PACK ORDERLY
Discipline is a form of training that brings order to life. For example, military discipline is what allows the soldiers in an army to work as one. Discipline is a form of teaching and, in dogs, is the basis of how the successful pack operates. Each member knows his place in the pack and all respect the leader, or Alpha dog. It is essential for your puppy that you establish this type of relationship, with you as the Alpha, or leader. It is a form of social coexistence that all canines recognize and accept. Discipline, therefore, is never to be confused with punishment. When you

teach your puppy how you want him to behave, and he behaves properly and you praise him for it, you are disciplining him with a form of positive reinforcement.

For a dog, rewards come in the form of praise, a smile, a cheerful tone of voice, a few friendly pats or a rub of the ears. Rewards are also small food treats. Obviously, that does not mean bits of regular dog food. Instead, treats are very small bits of special things like cheese or pieces of soft dog treats. The idea is to reward the dog with something very small that he can taste and swallow, providing instant positive reinforcement. If he has to take time to chew the treat, by the time he is finished he will have forgotten what he did to earn it!

Your puppy should never be physically punished. The displeasure shown on your face and in your voice is sufficient to signal to the pup that he has done something wrong. He wants to please everyone higher up on the social ladder, especially his leader, so a scowl and harsh voice will take care of the error. Growling out the word "Shame!" when the pup is caught in the act of doing something wrong is better than the repetitive "No." Some dogs hear "No" so often that they begin to think it's their name! By the way, do not use the dog's name when you're correcting him.

All work and no play makes your Wheaten a dull pup! Your puppy should have time to play as well as time to learn his lessons.

His name is reserved to get his attention for something pleasant about to take place.

There are punishments that have nothing to do with you. For example, your dog may think that chasing cats is one reason for his existence. You can try to stop it as much as you like but without success, because it's such fun for the dog. But one good hissing, spitting, swipe of a cat's claws across the dog's nose will put an end to the game forever. Intervene only when your dog's eyeball is seriously at risk. Cat scratches can cause permanent damage to an innocent but annoying puppy.

PUPPY KINDERGARTEN

COLLAR AND LEASH
Before you begin your SCWT puppy's education, he must be used to his collar and leash.

WHO'S TRAINING WHOM?

Dog training is a black-and-white exercise. The correct response to a command must be absolute, and the trainer must insist on completely accurate responses from the dog. A trainer cannot command his dog to sit and then settle for the dog's melting into the down position. Often owners are so pleased that their dogs "did something" in response to a command that they just shrug and say, "OK, Down" even though they wanted the dog to sit. You want your dog to respond to the command without hesitation: he must respond at that moment and correctly every time.

Choose a collar for your puppy that is secure, but not heavy or bulky. He won't enjoy training if he's uncomfortable. A flat buckle collar is fine for everyday wear and for initial puppy training. For older dogs, there are several types of training collars such as the martingale, which is a double loop that tightens slightly around the neck, or the head collar, which is similar to a horse's halter. Do not use a chain choke collar unless you have been specifically shown how to put it on and how to use it. You may not be disposed to use a chain choke collar even if your breeder has told you that it's suitable for your SCWT.

A lightweight 6-foot woven cotton or nylon training leash is preferred by most trainers because it is easy to fold up in your hand and comfortable to hold because there is a certain amount of give to it. There are lessons where the dog will start off 6 feet away from you at the end of the leash. The leash used to take the puppy outside to relieve himself is shorter because you don't want him to roam away from his area. The shorter leash will also be the one to use when you walk the puppy.

If you've been fortunate enough to enroll in a Puppy Kindergarten Training class, suggestions will be made as to the best collar and leash for your young puppy. I say "fortunate" because your puppy will be in a class with puppies in his age range (up to five months old) of all breeds and sizes. It's the perfect way for him to learn the right way (and the wrong way) to interact with other dogs as well as their people. You cannot teach your puppy how to interpret another dog's sign language. For a first-time puppy owner, these socialization classes are invaluable. For experienced dog owners, they are a real boon to further training.

ATTENTION

You've been using the dog's name since the minute you collected him from the breeder, so you should be able to get his attention by saying his name—with a big smile and in an excited tone of voice. His response will be the puppy equivalent of "Here I am! What are we going to do?" Your immediate response (if you haven't guessed by now) is "Good dog." Rewarding him at the

moment he pays attention to you teaches him the proper way to respond when he hears his name.

EXERCISES FOR A BASIC CANINE EDUCATION

THE SIT EXERCISE

There are several ways to teach the puppy to sit. The first one is to catch him whenever he is about to sit and, as his backside nears the floor, say "Sit, good dog!" That's positive reinforcement and, if your timing is sharp, he will learn that what he's doing at that second is connected to your saying "Sit" and that you think he's clever for doing it!

Another method is to start with the puppy on his leash in front of you. Show him a treat in the palm of your right hand. Bring your hand up under his nose and, almost in slow motion, move your hand up and back so his nose goes up in the air and his head tilts back as he follows the treat in

Chewing is entirely normal for puppies, but not everything in your home is normally chewable. Provide safe chew toys, and use proper disciplinary techniques to steer your SCWT into chewing only those toys.

"SCHOOL" MODE

When is your puppy ready for a lesson? Maybe not always when you are. Attempting training with treats just before his mealtime is asking for disaster. Notice what times of day he performs best and make that Fido's school time.

The beginning of the down command, with the dog at the trainer's left side and the trainer using the left hand to grasp the leash above and close to the dog's collar.

on your left side. Puppies generally do not appreciate this physical dominance.

After a few times, you should be able to show the dog a treat in the open palm of your hand, raise your hand waist-high as you say "Sit" and have him sit. Therefore, you have taught him two things at the same time. Both the verbal command and the motion of the hand are signals for the sit. Your puppy is watching you almost more than he is listening to you, so what you do is just as important as what you say.

Don't save any of these drills only for training sessions. Use them as much as possible at odd times during a normal day. The dog should always sit before being given his food dish. He should sit to let you go through a doorway first, when the doorbell rings or when you stop to speak to someone on the street.

THE DOWN EXERCISE

Before beginning to teach the down command, you must consider how the dog feels about this exercise. To him, "down" is a submissive position. Being flat on the floor with you standing over him is not his idea of fun. It's up to you to let him know that, while it may not be fun, the reward of your approval is worth his effort.

Start with the puppy on your left side in a sit position. Hold the leash right above his collar in

your hand. At that point, he will have to either sit or fall over, so as his back legs buckle under, say "Sit, good dog," and then give him the treat and lots of praise. You may have to begin with your hand lightly running up his chest, actually lifting his chin up until he sits. Some (usually older) dogs require gentle pressure on their hindquarters with the left hand, in which case the dog should be

your left hand. Have an extra-special treat, such as a small piece of cooked chicken or hot dog, in your right hand. Place it at the end of the pup's nose and steadily move your hand down and forward along the ground. Hold the leash to prevent a sudden lunge for the food. As the puppy goes into the down position, say "Down" very gently.

The difficulty with this exercise is twofold: it's both the submissive aspect and the fact that most people say the word "Down" as if they were a drill sergeant in charge of recruits. So issue the command sweetly, give him the treat and have the pup maintain the down position for several seconds. If he tries to get up immediately, place your hands on his shoulders and press down gently, giving him a very quiet "Good dog." As you progress with this lesson, increase the "down time" until he will hold it until you say "Okay" (his cue for release). Practice this one in the house at various times throughout the day.

By increasing the length of time during which the dog must maintain the down position, you'll find many uses for it. For example, he can lie at your feet in the vet's office or anywhere that both of you have to wait, when you are on the phone, while the family is eating and so forth. If you progress to training for competitive obedience, he'll

already be all set for the exercise called the "long down."

THE STAY EXERCISE
You can teach your SCWT to stay in the sit, down and stand positions. To teach the sit/stay, have the dog sit on your left side. Hold the leash at waist level in your left hand and let the dog

The result of a productive session of training to the down command. The down command requires continued reinforcement.

DOWN
"Down" is a harsh-sounding word and a submissive posture in dog body language, thus presenting two obstacles in teaching the down command. When the dog is about to flop down on his own, tell him "Good down." Pups that are not good about being handled learn better by lowering food in front of them. A dog that trusts you can be gently guided into position. When you give the command "Down," be sure to say it sweetly!

Your hand extended like a stop sign indicates for the dog to stay. The dog can be taught to stay in the sit position as well as the down and stand positions.

This Wheaten willingly assumes the down position as the handler uses a hand signal.

know that you have a treat in your closed right hand. Step forward on your right foot as you say "Stay." Immediately turn and stand directly in front of the dog, keeping your right hand up high so he'll keep his eye on the treat hand and maintain the sit position for a count of five. Return to your original position and offer the reward.

Increase the length of the sit/stay each time until the dog can hold it for at least 30 seconds without moving. After about a week of success, move out on

your right foot and take two steps before turning to face the dog. Give the "Stay" hand signal (left palm back toward the dog's head) as you leave. He gets the treat when you return and he holds the sit/stay. Increase the distance that you walk away from him before turning until you reach the length of your training leash. But don't rush it! Go back to the beginning if he moves before he should. No matter what the lesson, never be upset by having to back up for a few days. The repetition and practice are what will make your dog reliable in these commands. It won't do any good to move on to something more difficult if the command is not mastered at the easier levels. Above all, even if you do get frustrated, never let

your puppy know. Always keep a positive, upbeat attitude during training, which will transmit to your dog for positive results.

The down/stay is taught in the same way once the dog is completely reliable and steady with the down command. Again, don't rush it. With the dog in the down position on your left side, step out on your right foot as you say "Stay." Return by walking around in back of the dog and into your original position. While you are training, it's okay to murmur something like "Hold on" to encourage him to stay put. When the dog will stay without moving when you are at a distance of 3 or 4 feet, begin to increase the length of time before you return. Be sure he holds the down on your return until you say "Okay." At that point, he gets his treat—just so

With the leash held at waist level in the left hand, the treat-holding right hand maintains the dog's attention.

Your dog's proper execution of the stay command is an exercise in good canine manners and can be useful in everyday life.

COME AND GET IT!

The come command is your dog's safety signal. Until he is 99% perfect in responding, don't use the come command if you cannot enforce it. Practice on leash with treats or squeakers, or whenever the dog is running to you. Never call him to come to you if he is to be corrected for a misdemeanor. Reward the dog with a treat and happy praise whenever he comes to you.

he'll remember for next time that it's not over until it's over.

Treats are invaluable aids in training and are effective to convince your Wheaten pup to pay attention to its lesson.

THE COME EXERCISE

No command is more important to the safety of your SCWT than "Come." It is what you should say every single time you see the puppy running toward you: "Binky, come! Good dog." During playtime, run a few feet away from the puppy and turn and tell him to "Come" as he is already running to you. You can go so far as to teach your puppy two things at once if you squat down and hold out your arms. As the pup gets close to you and you're saying "Good dog," bring your right arm in about waist high. Now he's also learning the hand signal, an excellent device should you be on the phone when you need to get him to come to you. You'll also both be one step ahead when you enter obedience classes.

Puppies, like children, have notoriously short attention spans, so don't overdo it with any of the training. Keep each lesson short. Break it up with a quick run around the yard or a ball toss, repeat the lesson and quit as soon as the pup gets it right. That way, you will always end with a "Good dog."

When the puppy responds to your well-timed "Come," try it with the puppy on the training leash. This time, catch him off guard, while he's sniffing a leaf or watching a bird: "Binky, come!" You may have to pause for a split

second after his name to be sure you have his attention. If the puppy shows any sign of confusion, give the leash a mild jerk and take a couple of steps backward. Do not repeat the command. In this case, you should say "Good come" as he reaches you.

That's the number-one rule of training. Each command word is given just once. Anything more is nagging. You'll also notice that all commands are one word only. Even when they are actually two words, you say them as one.

Never call the dog to come to you—with or without his name—if you are angry or intend to correct him for some misbehavior. When correcting the pup, you go to him. Your dog must always connect "come" with something pleasant and with your approval; then you can rely on his response.

Life isn't perfect and neither are puppies. A time will come, often around 10 months of age, when he'll become "selectively deaf" or choose to "forget" his name. He may respond by wagging his tail (and even seeming to smile at you) with a look that says "Make me!" Laugh, throw his favorite toy and skip the lesson you had planned. Pups will be pups!

THE HEEL EXERCISE

The second most important command to teach, after the come, is the heel. When you are walking your growing puppy, you need to

> ### BE UPSTANDING!
> You are the dog's leader. During training, stand up straight so your dog looks up at you, and therefore up *to* you. Say the command words distinctly, in a clear, declarative tone of voice. (No barking!) Give rewards only as the correct response takes place (remember your timing!). Praise, smiles and treats are "rewards" used to positively reinforce correct responses. Don't repeat a mistake. Just change to another exercise—you will soon find success!

The heel lesson is under way as the handler proceeds slowly, making sure that her Wheaten keeps pace in the correct position.

dog on your left side. He will be in a very nice sit and you will have the training leash across your chest. Hold the loop and folded leash in your right hand. Pick up the slack leash above the dog in your left hand and hold it loosely at your side. Step out on your left foot as you say "Heel." If the puppy does not move, give a gentle tug or pat your left leg to get him started. If he surges ahead of you, stop and pull him back gently until he is at your side. Tell him to sit and begin again.

Walk a few steps and stop while the puppy is correctly beside you. Tell him to sit and give mild verbal praise. (More enthusiastic praise will encourage him to think the lesson is over.) Repeat the lesson, increasing the number of steps you take only as long as the dog is heeling nicely beside you. When you end the lesson, have him hold the sit, then

be in control. Besides, it looks terrible to be pulled and yanked down the street, and it's not much fun either. Your eight-to ten-week-old puppy will probably follow you everywhere, but that's his natural instinct, not your control over the situation. However, any time he does follow you, you can say "Heel" and be ahead of the game, as he will learn to associate this command with the action of following you before you even begin teaching him to heel.

There is a very precise, almost military, procedure for teaching your dog to heel. As with all other obedience training, begin with the

LET'S GO!
Many people use "Let's go" instead of "Heel" when teaching their dogs to behave on lead. It sounds more like fun! When beginning to teach the heel, whatever command you use, always step off on your left foot. That's the one next to the dog, who is on your left side, in case you've forgotten. Keep a loose leash. When the dog pulls ahead, stop, bring him back and begin again. Use treats to guide him around turns.

give him the "Okay" to let him know that this is the end of the lesson. Praise him so that he knows he did a good job.

The cure for excessive pulling (a common problem) is to stop when the dog is no more than 2 or 3 feet ahead of you. Guide him back into position and begin again. With a really determined puller, try switching to a head collar. This will automatically turn the pup's head toward you so you can bring him back easily to the heel position. Give quiet, reassuring praise every time the leash goes slack and he's staying with you.

Staying and heeling can take a lot out of a dog, so provide playtime and free-running exercise to shake off the stress when the lessons are over. You don't want him to associate training with all work and no fun.

TAPERING OFF TIDBITS

Your dog has been watching you—and the hand that treats— throughout all of his lessons, and now it's time to break the treat habit. Begin by giving him treats at the end of each lesson only. Then start to give a treat after the end of only some of the lessons. At the end of every lesson, as well as during the lessons, be consistent with the praise. Your pup now doesn't know whether he'll get a treat or not, but he should keep performing well just in case!

FROM HEEL TO ETERNITY

To begin, step away from the dog, who is in the sit position. Turn and stand directly in front of him so he won't be tempted to follow. Two seconds is a long, long time to your dog, so increase the time for which he's expected to stay only in short increments. Don't force it. When practicing the heel exercise, your dog will sit at your side whenever you stop. Don't stop for more than three seconds, as your enthusiastic dog will really feel that it's an eternity!

Finally, you will stop giving treat rewards entirely. Save them for something brand-new that you want to teach him. Keep up the praise and you'll always have a "good dog."

MORE PRAISE, LESS FOOD

As you progress with your puppy's lessons, and the puppy is responding well, gradually begin to wean him off the treats by alternating the treats with times when you offer only verbal praise or a few pats on the dog's side. (Pats on the head are dominant actions, so he won't think they are meant to be praise.) Every lesson should end with the puppy's performing the correct action for that session's command. When he gets it right and you withhold the treat, the praise can be as long and lavish as you like. The commands are one word only, but your verbal praise can use as many words as you want...don't skimp!

OBEDIENCE CLASSES

The advantages of an obedience class are that your dog will have to learn amid the distractions of other people and dogs and that your mistakes will be quickly corrected by the trainer. Teaching your dog along with a qualified instructor and other handlers who may have more dog experience than you is another plus of the class environment. The instructor and other handlers can help you to find the most efficient way of teaching your dog a command or exercise. It's often easier to learn by other people's mistakes than your own. You will also learn all of the requirements for competitive obedience trials, in which you can earn titles and go on to advanced jumping and retrieving exercises, which are fun for many dogs. Obedience classes build the foundation needed for many other canine activities (in which we humans are allowed to participate, too!).

TRAINING FOR OTHER ACTIVITIES

Once your dog has basic obedience under his collar and is 12 months of age, you can enter the world of agility training. Dogs think agility is pure fun, like being turned loose in an amusement park full of obstacles! In addition to agility, there are hunting activities for sporting dogs, lure-coursing events for sighthounds, go-to-ground events for terriers, racing for the Nordic sled dogs, herding trials for the shepherd breeds and tracking, which is open to all "nosey" dogs (which would include all dogs!). For those who like to volunteer, there is the wonderful feeling of owning a Therapy Dog and visiting hospices, nursing homes and veterans' homes to bring smiles, comfort and companionship to those who live there.

Around the house, your SCWT can be taught to do some

RIGHT CLICK ON YOUR DOG

With three clicks, the dolphin jumps through the hoop. Wouldn't it be nice to have a dog who could obey wordless commands that easily? Clicker training actually was developed by dolphin trainers and today is used on dogs with great success. You can buy a clicker at a pet shop or pet-supply outlet, and then you'll be off and clicking.

You can click your dog into learning new commands, shaping or conditioning his behavior and solving bad habits. The clicker, used in conjunction with a treat, is an extension of positive reinforcement. The dog begins to recognize your happy clicking, and you will never have to use negative reinforcement again. The dog is conditioned to follow your hand with the clicker, just as he would follow your hand with a treat. To discourage the dog from inappropriate behavior (like jumping up or barking), you can use the clicker to set a timeframe and then click and reward the dog once he's waited the allotted time without jumping up or barking.

simple chores. You might teach him to carry a basket of household items or to fetch the morning newspaper. The kids can teach the dog all kinds of tricks, from playing hide-and-seek to balancing a biscuit on his nose. A family dog is what rounds out the family. Everything he does beyond sitting in your lap or gazing lovingly at you represents the bonus of owning a dog.

Basic obedience commands are used in obedience competition. This Wheaten is sit-staying with a dumbbell at an obedience show.

Your Wheaten puppy relies upon you and your responsible education to keep him healthy and happy.

HEALTHCARE OF YOUR
SOFT COATED WHEATEN TERRIER

By Lowell Ackerman DVM, DACVD

HEALTHCARE FOR A LIFETIME
When you own a dog, you become his healthcare advocate over his entire lifespan, as well as being the one to shoulder the financial burden of such care. Accordingly, it is worthwhile to focus on prevention rather than treatment, as you and your pet will both be happier.

Of course, the best place to have begun your program of preventive healthcare is with the initial purchase or adoption of your dog. There is no way of guaranteeing that your new furry friend is free of medical problems, but there are some things you can do to improve your odds. You certainly should have done adequate research into the SCWT and have selected your puppy carefully rather than buying on impulse. Health issues aside, a large number of pet abandonment and relinquishment cases arise from a mismatch between pet needs and owner expectations. This is entirely preventable with appropriate planning and finding a good breeder.

The health of your SCWT, from puppyhood to the senior years, is in your arms!

Regarding healthcare issues specifically, it is very difficult to make blanket statements about where to acquire a problem-free pet, but, again, a reputable breeder is your best bet. In an ideal situation you have the opportunity to see both parents, get references from other owners of the breeder's pups and see genetic-testing documentation for several generations of the litter's ancestors. You will want to make certain that the breeder has screened for PRA, Addison's disease, RD, PLE and PLN. Genetic testing offers some important benefits, but testing is

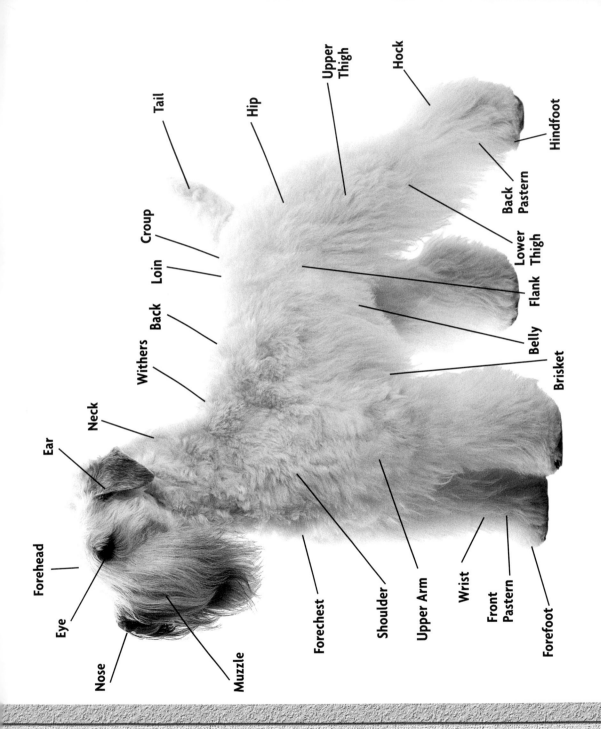

Forehead

Eye

Nose

Muzzle

Ear

Neck

Withers

Back

Loin

Croup

Tail

Hip

Upper Thigh

Hock

Hindfoot

Back Pastern

Lower Thigh

Flank

Belly

Brisket

Forechest

Shoulder

Upper Arm

Wrist

Front Pastern

Forefoot

PHYSICAL STRUCTURE OF THE SOFT COATED WHEATEN TERRIER

available for only a few disorders in a relatively small number of breeds and is not available for some of the most common genetic diseases, such as hip dysplasia, cataracts, epilepsy, cardiomyopathy, etc. This area of research is indeed exciting and increasingly important, and advances will continue to be made each year. In fact, recent research has shown that there is an equivalent dog gene for 75% of known human genes, so research done in either species is likely to benefit the other.

We've also discussed that evaluating the behavioral nature of your SCWT and that of his immediate family members is an important part of the selection process that cannot be underestimated or overemphasized. It is sometimes difficult to evaluate temperament in puppies because certain behavioral tendencies, such as some forms of aggression, may not be immediately evident. More dogs are euthanized each year for behavioral reasons than for all medical conditions combined, so it is critical to take temperament issues seriously. Start with a well-balanced, friendly companion and put the time and effort into proper socialization, and you will both be rewarded with a lifelong valued relationship.

Assuming that you have started off with a pup from healthy, sound stock, you then become responsible for helping your veterinarian keep your pet healthy. Some crucial things happen before you even bring your puppy home. Parasite control typically begins at two weeks of age, and vaccinations typically begin at six to eight weeks of age. A pre-pubertal evaluation is typically scheduled for about six months of age. At this time, a dental evaluation is done (since the adult teeth are now in), heartworm prevention is started and neutering or spaying is most commonly done.

It is critical to commence regular dental care at home if you have not already done so. It may not sound very important, but most dogs have active periodontal disease by four years of age if they don't have their teeth cleaned regularly at home, not just at their veterinary exams. Dental problems lead to more than just bad "doggie breath": gum disease can have very serious medical consequences. If you start brushing your dog's teeth and using antiseptic rinses from a young age, your dog will be accustomed to it and will not resist. The results will be healthy dentition, which your pet will need to enjoy a long, healthy life.

Most dogs are considered adults at a year of age, although some larger breeds still have some filling out to do up to about two or so years old. Even individual dogs

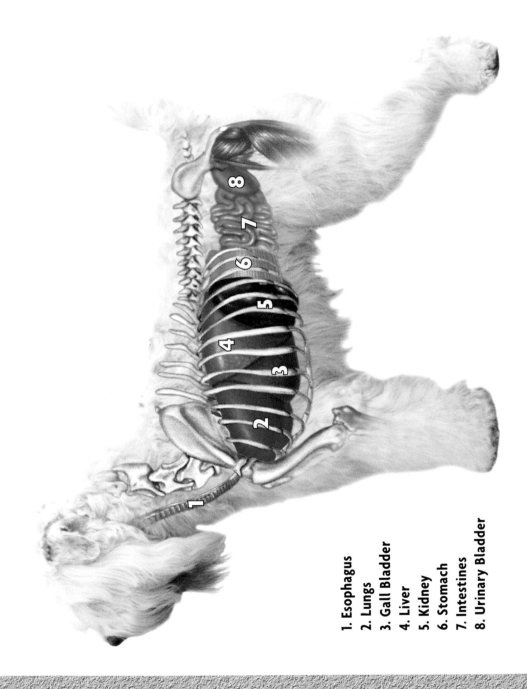

1. Esophagus
2. Lungs
3. Gall Bladder
4. Liver
5. Kidney
6. Stomach
7. Intestines
8. Urinary Bladder

INTERNAL ORGANS OF THE SOFT COATED WHEATEN TERRIER

within each breed have different healthcare requirements, so work with your veterinarian to determine what will be needed and what your role should be. This doctor-client relationship is important, because as vaccination guidelines change there may not be an annual "vaccine visit" scheduled. You must make sure that you see your veterinarian at least annually, even if no vaccines are due, because this is the best opportunity to coordinate health-care activities and to make sure that no medical issues creep by unaddressed.

When your SCWT reaches three-quarters of his anticipated lifespan, he is considered a "senior" and likely requires some special care. In general, if you've been taking great care of your canine companion throughout his formative and adult years, the transition to senior status should be a smooth one. Age is not a disease, and as long as everything is functioning as it should, there is no reason why most of late adulthood should not be rewarding for both you and your pet. This is especially true if you have tended to the details, such as regular veterinary visits, proper dental care, excellent nutrition and management of bone and joint issues.

At this stage in your SCWT's life, your veterinarian may want to schedule visits twice yearly,

TAKING YOUR DOG'S TEMPERATURE

It is important to know how to take your dog's temperature at times when you think he may be ill. It's not the most enjoyable task, but it can be done without too much difficulty. It's easier with a helper, preferably someone with whom the dog is friendly, so that one of you can hold the dog while the other inserts the thermometer.

Before inserting the thermometer, coat the end with petroleum jelly. Insert the thermometer slowly and gently into the dog's rectum about one inch. Wait for the reading, about two minutes. Be sure to remove the thermometer carefully and clean it thoroughly after each use.

A dog's normal body temperature is between 100.5 and 102.5 degrees F. Immediate veterinary attention is required if the dog's temperature is below 99 or above 104 degrees F.

instead of once, to run some laboratory screenings, electrocardiograms and the like, and to change the diet to something more digestible. Catching problems early is the best way to manage them effectively. Treating the early stages of heart disease is so much easier than trying to intervene when there is more significant damage to the heart muscle. Similarly, managing the beginning of kidney problems is fairly

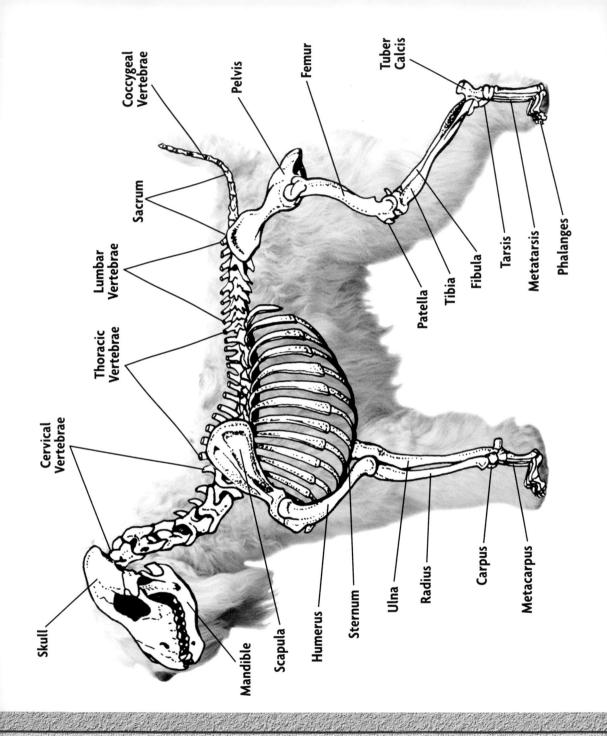

Coccygeal Vertebrae

Pelvis

Femur

Tuber Calcis

Sacrum

Lumbar Vertebrae

Thoracic Vertebrae

Cervical Vertebrae

Patella

Tibia

Fibula

Tarsis

Metatarsis

Phalanges

Skull

Mandible

Scapula

Humerus

Sternum

Ulna

Radius

Carpus

Metacarpus

SKELETAL STRUCTURE OF THE SOFT COATED WHEATEN TERRIER

routine if there is no significant kidney damage. Other problems, like cognitive dysfunction (similar to senility and Alzheimer's disease), cancer, diabetes and arthritis, are more common in older dogs, but all can be treated to help the dog live as many happy, comfortable years as possible. Just as in people, medical management is more effective (and less expensive) when you catch things early.

SELECTING A VETERINARIAN
There is probably no more important decision that you will make regarding your pet's health-care than the selection of his

doctor. Your pet's veterinarian will be a pediatrician, family-practice physician and gerontologist, depending on the dog's life stage, and will be the individual who makes recommendations regarding issues such as when specialists need to be consulted, when diagnostic testing and/or therapeutic intervention is needed and when you will need to seek outside emergency and critical-care services. Your vet will act as your advocate and liaison throughout these processes.

Everyone has his own idea about what to look for in a vet, an individual who will play a big role in his dog's (and, of course,

SAMPLE VACCINATION SCHEDULE

6-8 weeks of age	Parvovirus, Distemper, Adenovirus-2 (Hepatitis)
9-11 weeks of age	Parvovirus, Distemper, Adenovirus-2 (Hepatitis)
12-14 weeks of age	Parvovirus, Distemper, Adenovirus-2 (Hepatitis)
16-20 weeks of age	Rabies
1 year of age	Parvovirus, Distemper, Adenovirus-2 (Hepatitis), Rabies

Revaccination is performed every one to three years, depending on the product, the method of administration and the patient's risk. Initial adult inoculation (for dogs at least 16 weeks of age in which a puppy series was not done or could not be confirmed) is two vaccinations, done three to four weeks apart, with revaccination according to the same criteria mentioned. Other vaccines are given as decided between owner and veterinarian.

his own) life for many years to come. For some, it is the compassionate caregiver with whom they hope to develop a professional relationship to span the lifetime of their dogs and even their future pets. For others, they are seeking a clinician with keen diagnostic and therapeutic insight who can deliver state-of-the-art healthcare. Still others need a veterinary facility that is open evenings and weekends, or is in close proximity or provides mobile veterinary services, to accommodate their schedules; these people may not much mind that their dogs might see different veterinarians on each visit. Just as we have different reasons for selecting our own healthcare professionals (e.g., covered by insurance plan, expert in field, convenient location, etc.), we should not expect that there is a one-size-fits-all recommendation for selecting a veterinarian and veterinary practice. The best advice is to be honest in your assessment of what you expect from a veterinary practice and to conscientiously research the options in your area. You will

DISEASE REFERENCE CHART

	WHAT IS IT?	WHAT CAUSES IT?	SYMPTOMS
Leptospirosis	Severe disease that affects the internal organs; can be spread to people.	A bacterium, which is often carried by rodents, that enters through mucous membranes and spreads quickly throughout the body.	Range from fever, vomiting and loss of appetite in less severe cases to shock, irreversible kidney damage and possibly death in most severe cases.
Rabies	Potentially deadly virus that infects warm-blooded mammals.	Bite from a carrier of the virus, mainly wild animals.	1st stage: dog exhibits change in behavior, fear. 2nd stage: dog's behavior becomes more aggressive. 3rd stage: loss of coordination, trouble with bodily functions.
Parvovirus	Highly contagious virus, potentially deadly.	Ingestion of the virus, which is usually spread through the feces of infected dogs.	Most common: severe diarrhea. Also vomiting, fatigue, lack of appetite.
Canine cough	Contagious respiratory infection.	Combination of types of bacteria and virus. Most common: Bordetella bronchiseptica bacteria and parainfluenza virus.	Chronic cough.
Distemper	Disease primarily affecting respiratory and nervous system.	Virus that is related to the human measles virus.	Mild symptoms such as fever, lack of appetite and mucus secretion progress to evidence of brain damage, "hard pad."
Hepatitis	Virus primarily affecting the liver.	Canine adenovirus type I (CAV-1). Enters system when dog breathes in particles.	Lesser symptoms include listlessness, diarrhea, vomiting. More severe symptoms include "blue-eye" (clumps of virus in eye).
Coronavirus	Virus resulting in digestive problems.	Virus is spread through infected dog's feces.	Stomach upset evidenced by lack of appetite, vomiting, diarrhea.

quickly appreciate that not all veterinary practices are the same, and you will be happiest with one that truly meets your needs.

There is another point to be considered in the selection of veterinary services. Not that long ago, a single veterinarian would attempt to manage all medical and surgical issues as they arose. That was often problematic, because veterinarians are trained in many species and many diseases, and it was just impossible for general veterinary practitioners to be experts in every species, every field and every ailment. However, just as in the human healthcare fields, specialization has allowed general practitioners to concentrate on primary healthcare delivery, especially wellness and the prevention of infectious diseases, and to utilize a network of specialists to assist in the management of conditions that require specific expertise and experience. Thus there are now many types of veterinary specialists, including dermatologists, cardiologists, ophthalmologists, surgeons, internists, oncologists, neurologists, behaviorists, criticalists and others to help primary-care veterinarians deal with complicated medical challenges. In most cases, specialists see cases referred by primary-care veterinarians, make diagnoses and set up management plans. From there, the animals' ongoing care is returned to their primary-care veterinarians. This important team approach to your pet's medical-care needs has provided opportunities for advanced care and an unparalleled level of quality to be delivered.

With all of the opportunities for your SCWT to receive high-quality veterinary medical care, there is another topic that needs to be addressed at the same time— cost. It's been said that you can have excellent healthcare or inexpensive healthcare, but never both; this is as true in veterinary medicine as it is in human medicine. While veterinary costs are a fraction of what the same services cost in the human healthcare arena, it is still difficult to deal with unanticipated medical costs, especially since they can easily creep into hundreds or even

> ## DOGGIE DENTAL DON'TS
> A veterinary dental exam is necessary if you notice one or any combination of the following in your dog:
> - Broken, loose or missing teeth
> - Loss of appetite (which could be due to mouth pain or illness caused by infection)
> - Gum abnormalities, including redness, swelling and bleeding
> - Drooling, with or without blood
> - Yellowing of the teeth or gumline, indicating tartar
> - Bad breath.

thousands of dollars if specialists or emergency services become involved. However, there are ways of managing these risks. The easiest is to buy pet health insurance and realize that its foremost purpose is not to cover routine healthcare visits but rather to serve as an umbrella for those rainy days when your pet needs medical care and you don't want to worry about whether or not you can afford that care.

Pet insurance policies are very cost-effective (and very inexpensive by human health-insurance standards), but make sure that you buy the policy long before you intend to use it (preferably starting in puppyhood, because coverage will exclude pre-existing conditions) and that you are actually buying an indemnity

insurance plan from an insurance company that is regulated by your state or province. Many insurance policy look-alikes are actually discount clubs that are redeemable only at specific locations and for specific services. An indemnity plan covers your pet at almost all veterinary, specialty and emergency practices and is an excellent way to manage your pet's ongoing healthcare needs.

VACCINATIONS AND INFECTIOUS DISEASES

There has never been an easier time to prevent a variety of infectious diseases in your dog, but the advances we've made in veterinary medicine come with a price—choice. Now while it may seem that choice is a good thing (and it is), it has never been more

Every time you groom your Wheaten puppy, you should be inspecting for parasites or abnormalities of the skin and coat.

difficult for the pet owner (or the veterinarian) to make an informed decision about the best way to protect pets through vaccination.

Years ago, it was just accepted that puppies got a starter series of vaccinations and then annual "boosters" throughout their lives to keep them protected. As more and more vaccines became available, consumers wanted the convenience of having all of that protection in a single injection. The result was "multivalent" vaccines that crammed a lot of protection into a single syringe. The manufacturers' recommendations were to give the vaccines annually, and this was a simple enough protocol to follow. However, as veterinary medicine has become more sophisticated and we have started looking more at healthcare quandaries rather than convenience, it became necessary to reevaluate the situation and deal with some tough questions. It is important to realize that whether or not to use a particular vaccine depends on the risk of contracting the disease against which it protects, the severity of the disease if it is contracted, the duration of immunity provided by the vaccine, the safety of the product and the needs of the individual animal. In a very general sense, rabies, distemper, hepatitis and parvovirus are considered core vaccine needs, while

HIT ME WITH A HOT SPOT

What is a hot spot? Technically known as pyotraumatic dermatitis, a hot spot is an infection on the dog's coat, usually by the rear end, under the tail or on a leg, which the dog inflicts upon himself. The dog licks and bites the itchy spot until it becomes inflamed and infected. The hot spot can range in size from the circumference of a grape to the circumference of an apple. Provided that the hot spot is not related to a deeper bacterial infection, it can be treated topically by clipping the area, cleaning the sore and giving prednisone. For bacterial infections, antibiotics are required. In some cases, an Elizabethan collar is required to keep the dog from further irritating the hot spot. The itching can intensify and the pain becomes worse. Medicated shampoos and cool compresses, drying agents and topical steroids may be prescribed by your vet as well.

Hot spots can be caused by fleas, an allergy, an ear infection, anal sac problems, mange or a foreign irritant. Likewise, they can be linked to psychoses. The underlying problem must be addressed in addition to the hot spot itself.

parainfluenza, *Bordetella bronchiseptica*, leptospirosis, coronavirus and borreliosis (Lyme disease) are considered non-core needs and best reserved for animals that demonstrate reasonable risk of contracting the diseases.

NEUTERING/SPAYING

Sterilization procedures (neutering for males/spaying for females) are meant to accomplish several purposes. While the underlying premise is to address the risk of pet overpopulation, there are also some medical and behavioral benefits to the surgeries as well. For females, spaying prior to the first estrus (heat cycle) leads to a marked reduction in the risk of mammary cancer. There also will be no

Spaying/neutering is the best option for a companion dog. A responsible owner knows that her dog's life expectancy is increased by having her pet sterilized at a young age.

manifestations of "heat" to attract male dogs and no bleeding in the house. For males, there is prevention of testicular cancer and a reduction in the risk of prostate problems. In both sexes there may be some limited reduction in aggressive behaviors toward other dogs, and some diminishing of urine marking, roaming and mounting.

While neutering and spaying do indeed prevent animals from contributing to pet overpopulation, even no-cost and low-cost neutering options have not eliminated the problem. Perhaps one of the main reasons for this is that individuals who intentionally breed their dogs and those who allow their animals to run at large are the main causes of unwanted offspring. Also, animals in shelters are often there because they were abandoned or relinquished, not because they came from unplanned matings. Neutering/spaying is important, but it should be considered in the context of the real causes of animals' ending up in shelters and eventually being euthanized.

One of the important considerations regarding neutering is that it is a surgical procedure. This sometimes gets lost in discussions of low-cost procedures and commoditization of the process. In females, spaying is specifically referred to as an ovariohysterectomy. In this procedure, a midline incision is made in the abdomen and the entire uterus and both ovaries are surgically removed. While this is a major invasive surgical procedure, it usually has few complications, because it is typically performed on healthy young animals. However, it is major surgery, as any woman who has had a hysterectomy will attest.

In males, neutering has traditionally referred to castration, which involves the surgical removal of both testicles. While still a significant piece of surgery, there is not the abdominal exposure that is required in the female surgery. In addition, there is now a chemical sterilization option, in which a solution is injected into each testicle, leading to atrophy of the sperm-producing cells. This can typically be done under sedation rather than full anesthesia. This is a relatively new approach, and there are no long-term clinical studies yet available.

Neutering/spaying is typically done around six months of age at most veterinary hospitals, although techniques have been pioneered to perform the procedures in animals as young as eight weeks of age. In general, the surgeries on the very young animals are done for the specific reason of sterilizing them before they go to their new homes. This is done in some shelter hospitals for assurance that the animals will

SPAY'S THE WAY
Although spaying a female dog qualifies as major surgery—an ovariohysterectomy, in fact—this procedure is regarded as routine when performed by a qualified veterinarian on a healthy dog. The advantages to spaying a bitch are many and great. Spayed dogs do not develop uterine cancer or any life-threatening diseases of the genitals. Likewise, spayed dogs are at a significantly reduced risk of breast cancer. Bitches (and owners) are relieved of the demands of heat cycles. A spayed bitch will not leave bloody stains on your furniture during estrus, and you will not have to contend with single-minded macho males trying to climb your fence in order to seduce her. The spayed bitch's coat will not show the ill effects of her estrogen level's climbing such as a dull, lackluster outer coat or patches of hairlessness.

definitely not produce any pups. Otherwise, these organizations need to rely on owners to comply with their wishes to have the animals "altered" at a later date, something that does not always happen.

There are some exciting immunocontraceptive "vaccines" currently under development, and there may be a time when contraception in pets will not require surgical procedures. We anxiously await these developments.

THE **ABCs** OF
Emergency Care

Abrasions

Clean wound with running water or 3% hydrogen peroxide. Pat dry with gauze and spray with antibiotic. Do not cover.

Animal Bites

Clean area with soap and saline solution or water. Apply pressure to any bleeding area. Apply antibiotic ointment.

Antifreeze Poisoning

Induce vomiting and take dog to the vet.

Bee Sting

Remove stinger and apply soothing lotion or cold compress; give antihistamine in proper dosage.

Bleeding

Apply pressure directly to wound with gauze or towel for five to ten minutes. If wound does not stop bleeding, wrap wound with gauze and adhesive tape.

Bloat/Gastric Torsion

Immediately take the dog to the vet or emergency clinic; phone from car. No time to waste.

Burns

Chemical: Bathe dog with water and pet shampoo. Rinse in saline solution. Apply antibiotic ointment.

Acid: Rinse with water. Apply one part baking soda, two parts water to affected area.

Alkali: Rinse with water. Apply one part vinegar, four parts water to affected area.

Electrical: Apply antibiotic ointment. Seek veterinary assistance immediately.

Choking

If the dog is on the verge of collapsing, wedge a solid object, such as the handle of screwdriver, between molars on one side of the mouth to keep mouth open. Pull tongue out. Use long-nosed pliers or fingers to remove foreign object. Do not push the object down the dog's throat. For small or medium dogs, hold dog upside down by hind legs and shake firmly to dislodge foreign object.

Chlorine Ingestion

With clean water, rinse the mouth and eyes. Give the dog water to drink; contact the vet.

Constipation

Feed dog 2 tablespoons bran flakes with each meal. Encourage drinking water. Mix 1/4 teaspoon mineral oil in dog's food.

Diarrhea

Withhold food for 12 to 24 hours. Feed dog anti-diarrheal with eyedropper. When feeding resumes, feed one part boiled hamburger, one part plain cooked rice, 1/4 to 3/4 cup four times daily.

Dog Bite

Snip away hair around puncture wound; clean with 3% hydrogen peroxide; apply tincture of iodine. If wound appears deep, take the dog to the vet.

Frostbite

Wrap the dog in a heavy blanket. Warm affected area with a warm bath for ten minutes. Red color to skin will return with circulation; if tissues are pale after 20 minutes, contact the vet.

Use a portable, durable container large enough to contain all items

Heat Stroke
Partially submerge the dog in cold water; if no response within ten minutes, contact the vet.

Hot Spots
Mix 2 packets Domeboro® with 2 cups water. Saturate cloth with mixture and apply to hot spots for 15-30 minutes. Apply antibiotic ointment. Repeat every six to eight hours.

Poisonous Plants
Wash affected area with soap and water. Cleanse with alcohol. For foxtail/grass, apply antibiotic ointment.

Rat Poison Ingestion
Induce vomiting. Keep dog calm, maintain dog's normal body temperature (use blanket or heating pad). Get to the vet for antidote.

Shock
Keep the dog calm and warm; call for veterinary assistance.

Snake Bite
If possible, bandage the area and apply pressure. If the area is not conducive to bandaging, use ice to control bleeding. Get immediate help from the vet.

Tick Removal
Apply flea and tick spray directly on tick. Wait one minute. Using tweezers or wearing plastic gloves, apply constant pull while grasping tick's body. Apply antibiotic ointment.

Vomiting
Restrict dog's water intake; offer a few ice cubes. Withhold food for next meal. Contact vet if vomiting persists longer than 24 hours.

DOG OWNER'S FIRST-AID KIT
- ❑ Gauze bandages/swabs
- ❑ Adhesive and non-adhesive bandages
- ❑ Antibiotic powder
- ❑ Antiseptic wash
- ❑ Hydrogen peroxide 3%
- ❑ Antibiotic ointment
- ❑ Lubricating jelly
- ❑ Rectal thermometer
- ❑ Nylon muzzle
- ❑ Scissors and forceps
- ❑ Eyedropper
- ❑ Syringe
- ❑ Anti-bacterial/fungal solution
- ❑ Saline solution
- ❑ Antihistamine
- ❑ Cotton balls
- ❑ Nail clippers
- ❑ Screwdriver/pen knife
- ❑ Flashlight
- ❑ Emergency phone numbers

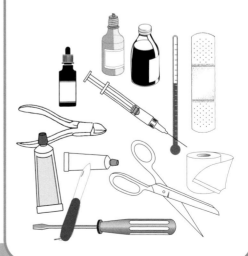

S. E. M. BY DR. DENNIS KUNKEL, UNIVERSITY OF HAWAII

A scanning electron micrograph of a dog flea, *Ctenocephalides canis*, on dog hair.

EXTERNAL PARASITES

FLEAS

Fleas have been around for millions of years and, while we have better tools now for controlling them than at any time in the past, there still is little chance that they will end up on an endangered species list. Actually, they are very well adapted to living on our pets, and they continue to adapt as we make advances.

The female flea can consume 15 times her weight in blood during active reproduction and can lay as many as 40 eggs a day. These eggs are very resistant to the effects of insecticides. They hatch into larvae, which then mature and spin cocoons. The immature fleas reside in this pupal stage until the time is right for feeding. This pupal stage is also very resistant to the effects of insecticides, and pupae can last in the environment without feeding for many months. Newly emergent fleas are attracted to animals by the warmth of the animals' bodies, movement and exhaled carbon dioxide. However, when they first emerge from their cocoons, they orient towards light; thus, when an animal passes between a flea and the light source, casting a shadow, the flea pounces and starts to feed. If the animal turns out to be a dog or cat, the reproductive cycle continues. If the flea lands on another type of animal, including a person, the flea will bite but will then look for a more appropriate host. An emerging adult flea can survive without feeding for up to 12 months but, once it tastes blood, it can only survive off its host for three to four days.

It was once thought that fleas spend most of their lives in the environment, but we now know that fleas won't willingly jump off a dog unless leaping to another dog or when physically removed by brushing, bathing or other manipulation. Flea eggs, on the other hand, are shiny and smooth, and they roll off the animal and into the environment. The eggs, larvae and pupae then exist in the environment, but once the adult finds a susceptible animal, it's home sweet home until the flea is forced to seek refuge elsewhere.

Since adult fleas live on the animal and immature forms survive in the environment, a successful treatment plan must address all stages of the flea life cycle. There are now several safe and effective flea-control products that can be applied on a monthly

FLEA PREVENTION FOR YOUR DOG

- Discuss with your veterinarian the safest product to protect your dog, likely in the form of a monthly tablet or a liquid preparation placed on the back of the dog's neck.
- For dogs suffering from flea-bite dermatitis, a shampoo or topical insecticide treatment is required.
- Your lawn and property should be sprayed with an insecticide designed to kill fleas and ticks that lurk outdoors.
- Using a flea comb, check the dog's coat regularly for any signs of parasites.
- Practice good housekeeping. Vacuum floors, carpets and furniture regularly, especially in the areas that the dog frequents, and wash the dog's bedding weekly.
- Follow up house-cleaning with carpet shampoos and sprays to rid the house of fleas at all stages of development. Insect growth regulators are the safest option.

basis. These include fipronil, imidacloprid, selamectin and permethrin (found in several formulations). Most of these products have significant flea-killing rates within 24 hours. However, none of them will control the immature forms in the environment. To accomplish this, there are a variety of insect growth regulators that can be

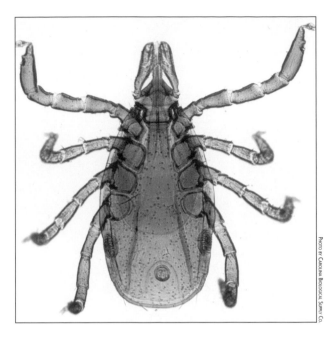

Deer tick,
Ixodes dammini.

PHOTO BY CAROLINA BIOLOGICAL SUPPLY CO.

which may be deeply embedded in the skin. This is best accomplished with forceps designed especially for this purpose; fingers can be used but should be protected with rubber gloves, plastic wrap or at least a paper towel. The tick should be grasped as closely as possible to the animal's skin and should be pulled upward with steady, even pressure. Do not squeeze, crush or puncture the body of the tick or you risk exposure to any disease carried by that tick. Once the ticks have been removed, the sites of attachment should be disinfected. Your hands should then be washed with soap and water to further minimize risk of contagion. The tick should be disposed of in a container of alcohol or household bleach.

Some of the newer flea products, specifically those with fipronil, selamectin and permethrin, have effect against some, but not all, species of tick. Flea collars containing appropriate pesticides (e.g., propoxur, chlorfenvinphos) can aid in tick control. In most areas, such collars should be placed on animals in March, at the beginning of the tick season, and changed regularly. Leaving the collar on when the pesticide level is waning invites the development of resistance. Amitraz collars are also good for tick control, and the active ingredient does not interfere with other flea-control products. The ingredient helps prevent the attachment of ticks to the skin and will cause those ticks already on the skin to detach themselves.

TICK CONTROL

Removal of underbrush and leaf litter and the thinning of trees in areas where tick control is desired are recommended. These actions remove the cover and food sources for small animals that serve as hosts for ticks. With continued mowing of grasses in these areas, the probability of ticks' surviving is further reduced. A variety of insecticide ingredients (e.g., resmethrin, carbaryl, permethrin, chlorpyrifos, dioxathion and allethrin) are registered for tick control around the home.

MITES

Mites are tiny arachnid parasites that parasitize the skin of dogs. Skin diseases caused by mites are referred to as "mange," and there are many different forms seen in dogs. These forms are very different from one another, each one warranting an individual description.

Sarcoptic mange, or scabies, is one of the itchiest conditions that affects dogs. The microscopic *Sarcoptes* mites burrow into the superficial layers of the skin and can drive dogs crazy with itchiness. They are also communicable to people, although they can't complete their reproductive cycle on people. Not only are the mites tiny but also are often difficult to find when trying to make a diagnosis. Skin scrapings from multiple areas are examined microscopically but, even then, sometimes the mites cannot be found.

Fortunately, scabies is relatively easy to treat, and there are a variety of products that will successfully kill the mites. Since the mites can't live in the environment for very long without feeding, a complete cure is usually possible within four to eight weeks.

Cheyletiellosis is caused by a relatively large mite, which sometimes can be seen even without a microscope. Often referred to as "walking dandruff," this also causes itching, but not usually as profound as with scabies.

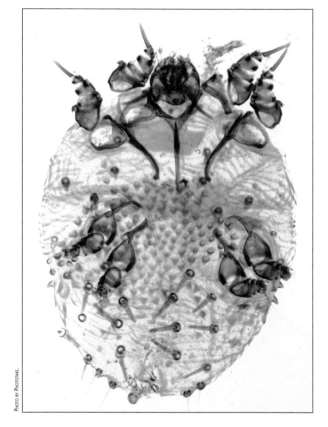

PHOTO BY PHOTOTAKE.

Sarcoptes scabiei, commonly known as the "itch mite."

While *Cheyletiella* mites can survive somewhat longer in the environment than scabies mites, they too are relatively easy to treat, being responsive to not only the medications used to treat scabies but also often to flea-control products.

Otodectes cynotis is the name of the ear mite and is one of the more common causes of mange, especially in young dogs in shelters or pet stores. That's because the mites are typically present in large numbers and are quickly spread to

Micrograph of a dog louse, *Heterodoxus spiniger*. Female lice attach their eggs to the hairs of the dog. As the eggs hatch, the larval lice bite and feed on the blood. Lice can also feed on dead skin and hair. This feeding activity can cause hair loss and skin problems.

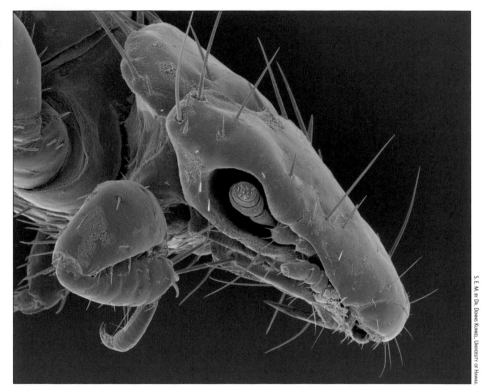

S. E. M. BY DR. DENNIS KUNKEL, UNIVERSITY OF HAWAII.

nearby animals. The mites rarely do much harm but can be difficult to eradicate if the treatment regimen is not comprehensive. While many try to treat the condition with ear drops only, this is the most common cause of treatment failure. Ear drops cause the mites to simply move out of the ears and as far away as possible (usually to the base of the tail) until the insecticide levels in the ears drop to an acceptable level—then it's back to business as usual! The successful treatment of ear mites requires treating all animals in the household with a systemic insecticide, such as selamectin, or a combination of miticidal ear drops combined with whole-body flea-control preparations.

Demodicosis, sometimes referred to as red mange, can be one of the most difficult forms of mange to treat. Part of the problem has to do with the fact that the mites live in the hair follicles and they are relatively well shielded from topical and systemic products. The main issue, however, is that demodectic mange typically results only when there is some underlying process interfering with the dog's immune system.

Since *Demodex* mites are

normal residents of the skin of mammals, including humans, there is usually a mite population explosion only when the immune system fails to keep the number of mites in check. In young animals, the immune deficit may be transient or may reflect an actual inherited immune problem. In older animals, demodicosis is usually seen only when there is another disease hampering the immune system, such as diabetes, cancer, thyroid problems or the use of immune-suppressing drugs. Accordingly, treatment involves not only trying to kill the mange mites but also discerning what is interfering with immune function and correcting it if possible.

Chiggers represent several different species of mite that don't parasitize dogs specifically, but do latch on to passersby and can cause irritation. The problem is most prevalent in wooded areas in the late summer and fall. Treatment is not difficult, as the mites do not complete their life cycle on dogs and are susceptible to a variety of miticidal products.

MOSQUITOES

Mosquitoes have long been known to transmit a variety of diseases to people, as well as just being biting pests during warm weather. They also pose a real risk to pets. Not only do they carry deadly heartworms but recently there also has been much concern over their involvement with West Nile virus. While we can avoid heartworm with the use of preventive medications, there are no such preventives for West Nile virus. The only method of prevention in endemic areas is active mosquito control. Fortunately, most dogs that have been exposed to the virus only developed flu-like symptoms and, to date, there have not been the large number of reported deaths in canines as seen in some other species.

ILLUSTRATION BY PHOTOTAKE

Illustration of Demodex folliculoram.

MOSQUITO REPELLENT

Low concentrations of DEET (less than 10%), found in many human mosquito repellents, have been safely used in dogs but, in these concentrations, probably give only about two hours of protection. DEET may be safe in these small concentrations, but since it is not licensed for use on dogs, there is no research proving its safety for dogs. Products containing permethrin give the longest-lasting protection, perhaps two to four weeks. As DEET is not licensed for use on dogs, and both DEET and permethrin can be quite toxic to cats, appropriate care should be exercised. Other products, such as those containing oil of citronella, also have some mosquito-repellent activity, but typically have a relatively short duration of action.

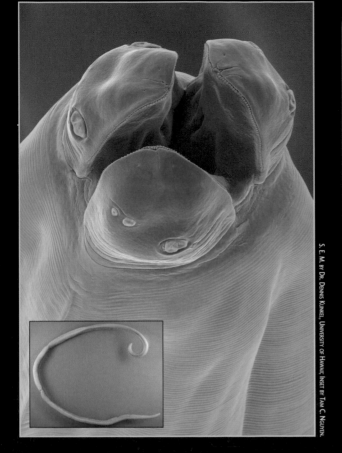

S. E. M. BY DR. DENNIS KUNKEL, UNIVERSITY OF HAWAII; INSET BY TAM C. NGUYEN.

ASCARID DANGERS

The most commonly encountered worms in dogs are roundworms known as ascarids. *Toxascaris leonine* and *Toxocara canis* are the two species that infect dogs. Subsisting in the dog's stomach and intestines, adult roundworms can grow to 7 inches in length and adult females can lay in excess of 200,000 eggs in a single day.

In humans, visceral larval migrans affects people who have ingested eggs of *Toxocara canis*, which frequently contaminates children's sandboxes, beaches and park grounds. The roundworms reside in the human's stomach and intestines, as they would in a dog's, but do not mature. Instead, they find their way to the liver, lungs and skin, or even to the heart or kidneys in severe cases. Deworming puppies is critical in preventing the infection in humans, and young children should never handle nursing pups who have not been dewormed.

The ascarid roundworm *Toxocara canis*, showing the mouth with three lips. INSET: Photomicrograph of the roundworm *Ascaris lumbricoides.*

INTERNAL PARASITES: WORMS

ASCARIDS

Ascarids are intestinal roundworms that rarely cause severe disease in dogs. Nonetheless, they are of major public health significance because they can be transferred to people. Sadly, it is children who are most commonly affected by the parasite, probably from inadvertently ingesting ascarid-contaminated soil. In fact, many yards and children's sandboxes contain appreciable numbers of ascarid eggs. So, while ascarids don't bite dogs or latch onto their intestines to suck blood, they do cause some nasty medical conditions in children and are best eradicated from our furry friends. Because pups can start passing ascarid eggs by three weeks of age, most parasite-control programs begin at two weeks of age and are repeated every two weeks until pups are eight weeks old. It is important to

S. E. M. BY DR. DENNIS KUNKEL, UNIVERSITY OF HAWAII.

realize that bitches can pass ascarids to their pups even if they test negative prior to whelping. Accordingly, bitches are best treated at the same time as the pups.

HOOKWORMS

Unlike ascarids, hookworms do latch onto a dog's intestinal tract and can cause significant loss of blood and protein. Similar to ascarids, hookworms can be transmitted to humans, where they cause a condition known as cutaneous larval migrans. Dogs can become infected either by consuming the infective larvae or by the larvae's penetrating the skin directly. People most often get infected when they are lying on the ground (such as on a beach) and the larvae penetrate the skin. Yes, the larvae can penetrate through a beach blanket. Hookworms are typically susceptible to the same medications used to treat ascarids.

The hookworm *Ancylostoma caninum* infects the colon of dogs. INSET: Note the row of hooks at the posterior end, used to anchor the worm to the intestinal wall.

WHIPWORMS

Whipworms latch onto the lower aspects of the dog's colon and can cause cramping and diarrhea. Eggs do not start to appear in the dog's feces until about three months after the dog was infected. This worm has a peculiar life cycle, which makes it more difficult to control than ascarids or hookworms. The good thing is that whipworms rarely are transferred to people.

Some of the medications used to treat ascarids and hookworms are also effective against whipworms, but, in general, a separate treatment protocol is needed. Since most of the medications are effective against the adults but not the eggs or larvae, treatment is typically repeated in three weeks, and then often in three months as well. Unfortunately,

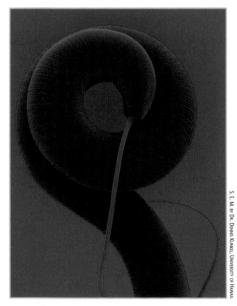

Adult whipworm, *Trichuris* sp., an intestinal parasite.

S. E. M. BY DR. DENNIS KUNKEL, UNIVERSITY OF HAWAII.

WORM-CONTROL GUIDELINES

- Practice sanitary habits with your dog and home.
- Clean up after your dog and don't let him sniff or eat other dogs' droppings.
- Control insects and fleas in the dog's environment. Fleas, lice, cockroaches, beetles, mice and rats can act as hosts for various worms.
- Prevent dogs from eating uncooked meat, raw poultry and dead animals.
- Keep dogs and children from playing in sand and soil.
- Kennel dogs on cement or gravel; avoid dirt runs.
- Administer heartworm preventives regularly.
- Have your vet examine your dog's stools at your annual visits.
- Select a boarding kennel carefully so as to avoid contamination from other dogs or an unsanitary environment.
- Prevent dogs from roaming. Obey local leash laws.

since dogs don't develop resistance to whipworms, it is difficult to prevent them from getting reinfected if they visit soil contaminated with whipworm eggs.

TAPEWORMS

There are many different species of tapeworm that affect dogs, but *Dipylidium caninum* is probably the most common and is spread by fleas. Flea larvae feed on organic debris and tapeworm eggs in the environment and, when a dog chews at himself and manages to ingest fleas, he might get a dose of tapeworm at the same time. The tapeworm then develops further in the intestine of the dog.

The tapeworm itself, which is a parasitic flatworm that latches onto the intestinal wall, is composed of numerous segments. When the segments break off into the intestine (as proglottids), they may accumulate around the rectum, like grains of rice. While this tapeworm is disgusting in its behavior, it is not directly communicable to humans (although humans can also get infected by swallowing fleas).

A much more dangerous flatworm is *Echinococcus multilocularis*, which is typically found in foxes, coyotes and wolves. The eggs are passed in the feces and infect rodents, and, when dogs eat the rodents, the dogs can be infected by thousands of adult tapeworms. While the parasites don't cause many problems in dogs, this is considered the most lethal worm infection that people can get. Take appropriate precautions if you live in an area in which these tapeworms are found. Do not use mulch that may contain feces of dogs, cats or wildlife, and discourage your pets from hunting

wildlife. Treat these tapeworm infections aggressively in pets, because if humans get infected, approximately half die.

HEARTWORMS

Heartworm disease is caused by the parasite *Dirofilaria immitis* and is seen in dogs around the world. The parasite itself, another nematode, is spread between dogs by the bite of an infected mosquito. The mosquito injects infective larvae into the dog's skin with its bite, and these larvae develop under the skin for a period of time before making their way to the heart. There they develop into adults, which grow and create blockages of the heart, lungs and major blood vessels there. They also start producing offspring (microfilariae)

The dog tapeworm proglottid (body segment).

The dog tapeworm *Taenia pisiformis*.

S. E. M. BY DR. DENNIS KUNKEL, UNIVERSITY OF HAWAII.

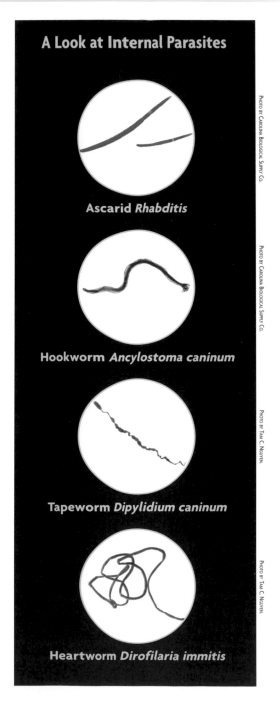

A Look at Internal Parasites

Ascarid *Rhabditis*

Photo by Carolina Biological Supply Co.

Hookworm *Ancylostoma caninum*

Photo by Carolina Biological Supply Co.

Tapeworm *Dipylidium caninum*

Photo by Tam C. Nguyen

Heartworm *Dirofilaria immitis*

Photo by Tam C. Nguyen

and these microfilariae circulate in the bloodstream, waiting to hitch a ride when the next mosquito bites. Once in the mosquito, the microfilariae develop into infective larvae and the entire process is repeated.

When dogs get infected with heartworm, over time they tend to develop symptoms associated with heart disease, such as coughing, exercise intolerance and potentially many other manifestations. Diagnosis is confirmed by either seeing the microfilariae themselves in blood samples or using immunologic tests (antigen testing) to identify the presence of adult heartworms. Since antigen tests measure the presence of adult heartworms and microfilarial tests measure offspring produced by adults, neither are positive until six to seven months after the initial infection. However, the beginning of damage can occur by fifth-stage larvae as early as three months after infection. Thus it is possible for dogs to be harboring problem-causing larvae for up to three months before either type of test would identify an infection.

The good news is that there are great protocols available for preventing heartworm in dogs. Testing is critical in the process, and it is important to understand the benefits as well as the limitations of such testing. All dogs six months of age or older that have not been on continuous heartworm-preventive medication should be

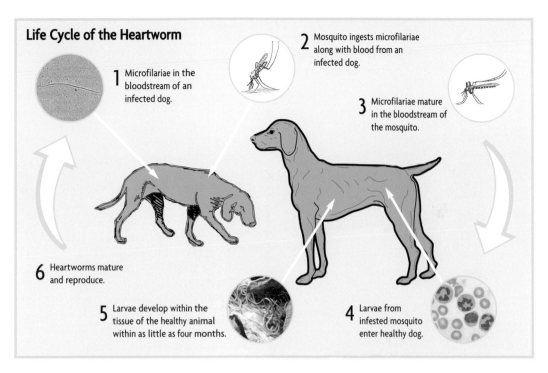

Life Cycle of the Heartworm

1 Microfilariae in the bloodstream of an infected dog.

2 Mosquito ingests microfilariae along with blood from an infected dog.

3 Microfilariae mature in the bloodstream of the mosquito.

4 Larvae from infested mosquito enter healthy dog.

5 Larvae develop within the tissue of the healthy animal within as little as four months.

6 Heartworms mature and reproduce.

screened with microfilarial or antigen tests. For dogs receiving preventive medication, periodic antigen testing helps assess the effectiveness of the preventives. The American Heartworm Society guidelines suggest that annual retesting may not be necessary when owners have absolutely provided continuous heartworm prevention. Retesting on a two- to three-year interval may be sufficient in these cases. However, your veterinarian will likely have specific guidelines under which heartworm preventives will be prescribed, and many prefer to err on the side of safety and retest annually.

It is indeed fortunate that heartworm is relatively easy to prevent, because treatments can be as life-threatening as the disease itself. Treatment requires a two-step process that kills the adult heartworms first and then the microfilariae. Prevention is obviously preferable; this involves a once-monthly oral or topical treatment. The most common oral preventives include ivermectin (not suitable for some breeds), moxidectin and milbemycin oxime; the once-a-month topical drug selamectin provides heartworm protection in addition to flea, tick and other parasite controls.

Number-One Killer Disease in Dogs: CANCER

In every age there is a word associated with a disease or plague that causes humans to shudder. In the 21st century, that word is "cancer." Just as cancer is the leading cause of death in humans, it claims nearly half the lives of dogs that die from a natural disease as well as half the dogs that die over the age of ten years.

Described as a genetic disease, cancer becomes a greater risk as the dog ages. Vets and dog owners have become increasingly aware of the threat of cancer to dogs. Statistics reveal that one dog in every five will develop cancer, the most common of which is skin cancer. Many cancers, including prostate, ovarian and breast cancer, can be avoided by spaying and neutering our dogs by the age of six months.

Early detection of cancer can save or extend a dog's life, so it is absolutely vital for owners to have their dogs examined by a qualified vet or oncologist immediately upon detection of any abnormality. Certain dietary guidelines have also proven to reduce the onset and spread of cancer. Foods based on fish rather than beef, due to the presence of Omega-3 fatty acids, are recommended. Other amino acids such as glutamine have significant benefits for canines, particularly those breeds that show a greater susceptibility to cancer.

Cancer management and treatments promise hope for future generations of canines. Since the disease is genetic, breeders should never breed a dog whose parents, grandparents and any related siblings have developed cancer. It is difficult to know whether to exclude an otherwise healthy dog from a breeding program, as the disease does not manifest itself until the dog's senior years.

RECOGNIZE CANCER WARNING SIGNS

Since early detection can possibly rescue your dog from becoming a cancer statistic, it is essential for owners to recognize the possible signs and seek the assistance of a qualified professional.

- Abnormal bumps or lumps that continue to grow
- Bleeding or discharge from any body cavity
- Persistent stiffness or lameness
- Recurrent sores or sores that do not heal
- Inappetence
- Breathing difficulties
- Weight loss
- Bad breath or odors
- General malaise and fatigue
- Eating and swallowing problems
- Difficulty urinating and defecating

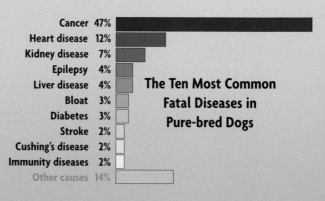

Disease	Percentage
Cancer	47%
Heart disease	12%
Kidney disease	7%
Epilepsy	4%
Liver disease	4%
Bloat	3%
Diabetes	3%
Stroke	2%
Cushing's disease	2%
Immunity diseases	2%
Other causes	14%

The Ten Most Common Fatal Diseases in Pure-bred Dogs

Recognizing a Sick Dog

Unlike colicky babies and cranky children, our canine kids cannot tell us when they are feeling ill. Therefore, there are a number of signs that owners can identify to know that their dogs are not feeling well.

**Take note of
physical manifestations such as:**

- unusual bad odor, including bad breath
- excessive shedding
- wax in the ears, chronic ear irritation
- oily, flaky, dull haircoat
- mucus, tearing or similar discharge in the eyes
- fleas or mites
- mucus in stool, diarrhea
- sensitivity to petting or handling
- licking at paws, scratching face, etc.

**Keep an eye out for
behavioral changes as well including:**

- lethargy, idleness
- lack of patience or general irritability
- lack of interest in food
- phobias (fear of people, loud noises, etc.)
- strange behavior, suspicion, fear
- coprophagia
- more frequent barking
- whimpering, crying

Get Well Soon

You don't need a DVM to provide good TLC to your sick or recovering dog, but you do need to pay attention to some details that normally wouldn't bother him. The following tips will aid Fido's recovery and get him back on his paws again:

- Keep his space free of irritating smells, like heavy perfumes and air fresheners.
- Rest is the best medicine! Avoid harsh lighting that will prevent your dog from sleeping. Shade him from bright sunlight during the day and dim the lights in the evening.
- Keep the noise level down. Animals are more sensitive to sound when they are sick.

- Be attentive to any necessary temperature adjustments. A dog with a fever needs a cool room and cold liquids. A bitch that is whelping or recovering from surgery will be more comfortable in a warm room, consuming warm liquids and food.
- You wouldn't send a sick child back to school early, so don't rush your dog back into a full routine until he seems absolutely ready.

Formal show training can yield *formal* successes for dog and owner. This handsome Wheaten is taking home the ribbon from a very large all-breed dog show.

SHOWING YOUR

SOFT COATED
WHEATEN TERRIER

Is dog showing in your blood? Are you excited by the idea of gaiting your handsome SCWT around the ring to the thunderous applause of an enthusiastic audience? Are you certain that your beloved SCWT is flawless? You are not alone! Every loving owner thinks that his dog has no faults, or too few to mention. No matter how many times an owner reads the breed standard, he cannot find any faults in his aristocratic companion dog. If this sounds like you, and if you are considering entering your SCWT in a dog show, here are some basic questions to ask yourself:

- Did you purchase a "show-quality" puppy from the breeder?
- Is your puppy at least six months of age?
- Does the puppy exhibit correct show type for his breed?
- Does your puppy have any disqualifying faults?
- Is your SCWT registered with the American Kennel Club?
- How much time do you have to devote to training, grooming,

There's no height the SCWT cannot reach. This Wheaten is clearing the "wall" at an agility trial.

conditioning and exhibiting your dog?
- Do you understand the rules and regulations of a dog show?
- Do you have time to learn how to show your dog properly?
- Do you have the financial resources to invest in showing your dog?
- Will you show the dog yourself or hire a professional handler?
- Do you have a vehicle that can accommodate your weekend trips to the dog shows?

Success in the show ring requires more than a pretty face, a waggy tail and a pocketful of liver. Even though dog shows can be

To present the dogs to their best advantage, handlers often help the dogs assume a flattering "stack," or show stance.

exciting and enjoyable, the sport of conformation makes great demands on the exhibitors and the dogs. Winning exhibitors live for their dogs, devoting time and money to their dogs' presentation, conditioning and training. Very few novices, even those with good dogs, will find themselves in the winners' circle, though it does happen. Don't be disheartened, though. Every exhibitor began as a novice and worked his way up to the Group ring. It's the "working your way up" part that you must keep in mind.

Assuming that you have purchased a puppy of the correct type and quality for showing, let's begin to examine the world of showing and what's required to get started. Although the entry

FOR MORE INFORMATION....

For reliable up-to-date information about registration, dog shows and other canine competitions, contact one of the national registries by mail or via the Internet.

American Kennel Club
5580 Centerview Dr., Raleigh, NC 27606-3390
www.akc.org

United Kennel Club
100 E. Kilgore Road, Kalamazoo, MI 49002
www.ukcdogs.com

Canadian Kennel Club
89 Skyway Ave., Suite 100, Etobicoke, Ontario
M9W 6R4 Canada
www.ckc.ca

The Kennel Club
1-5 Clarges St., Piccadilly, London W1Y 8AB, UK
www.the-kennel-club.org.uk

This lovely bitch is winning at the national specialty, held every year in conjunction with the famous Montgomery County all-Terrier show.

SHOW POTENTIAL

How possible is it to predict how your ten-week-old puppy will eventually do in the show ring? Most show dogs reach their prime at around three years of age, when their bodies are physically mature and their coats are in "full bloom." Experienced breeders, having watched countless pups grow into Best of Breed winners, recognize the glowing attributes that spell "show potential." When selecting a puppy for show, it's best to trust the breeder to recommend which puppy will best suit your aspirations. Some breeders recommend starting with a male puppy, which likely will be more "typey" than his female counterpart.

champion. Things like equipment, travel, training and conditioning all cost money. A more serious campaign will include fees for a professional handler, boarding, cross-country travel and advertising. Top-winning show dogs can represent a very considerable investment— over $100,000 has been spent in campaigning some dogs. (The investment can be less, of course, for owners who don't use professional handlers.)

Many owners, on the other hand, enter their "average" SCWTs in dog shows for the fun and enjoyment of it. Dog showing

fee into a dog show is nominal, there are lots of other hidden costs involved with "finishing" your SCWT, that is, making him a

makes an absorbing hobby, with many rewards for dogs and owners alike. If you're having fun, meeting other people who share your interests and enjoying the overall experience, you likely will catch the "bug." Once the dog-show bug bites, its effects can last a lifetime; it's certainly much better than a deer tick! Soon you will be envisioning yourself in the center ring at the Westminster Kennel Club Dog Show in New York City, competing for the prestigious Best in Show cup. This magical dog show is televised annually from Madison Square Garden,

The SCWT is lovable for itself alone, but a truly excellent example of the breed affords his owner an extra measure of pride.

and the victorious dog becomes a celebrity overnight.

AKC CONFORMATION SHOWING

GETTING STARTED

Visiting a dog show as a spectator is a great place to start. Pick up the show catalog to find out what time your breed is being shown, who is judging the breed and in which ring the classes will be held. To start, SCWTs compete against other SCWTs, and the winner is selected as Best of Breed by the judge. This is the procedure for each breed. At a group show, all of the Best of Breed winners go on to compete for Group One in their respective group. For example, all Best of Breed winners in a given group

The judge is asking the exhibitors to gait their dogs so that he can evaluate the dogs' movement.

compete against each other; this is done for all seven groups. Finally, all seven group winners go head to head in the ring for the Best in Show award.

What most spectators don't understand is the basic idea of conformation. A dog show is often referred as a "conformation" show. This means that the judge should decide how each dog stacks up (conforms) to the breed standard for his given breed: how well does this SCWT conform to the ideal representative detailed in the standard? Ideally, this is what happens. In reality, however, this ideal often gets slighted as the judge compares SCWT #1 to SCWT #2. Again, the ideal is that each dog is judged based on his merits in comparison to his breed standard, not in comparison to the other dogs in the ring. It is easier for judges to compare dogs of the same breed to decide which they think is the better specimen; in the Group and Best in Show ring, however, it is very difficult to compare one breed to another, like apples to oranges. Thus the dog's conformation to the breed standard—not to mention advertising dollars and good handling—is essential to success in conformation shows. The dog described in the standard (the standard for each AKC breed is written and approved by the breed's national parent club and then submitted to the AKC for

approval) is the perfect dog of that breed, and breeders keep their eye on the standard when they choose which dogs to breed, hoping to get closer and closer to the ideal with each litter.

Another good first step for the novice is to join a dog club. You will be astonished by the many and different kinds of dog clubs in the country, with about 5,000 clubs holding events every year. Most clubs require that prospective new members present two letters of recommendation from existing members. Perhaps you've made some friends visiting a show held by a particular club and you would like to join that club. Dog clubs may specialize in a single breed, like a local or regional SCWT club, or in a specific pursuit, such as obedience, tracking or hunting tests. There are all-breed clubs for all dog enthusiasts; they sponsor special training days, seminars on topics like grooming or handling or lectures on breeding or canine genetics. There are also clubs that specialize in certain types of dogs, like herding dogs, hunting dogs, companion dogs, etc.

A parent club is the national organization, sanctioned by the AKC, which promotes and safeguards its breed in the country. The SCWT Club of America was formed in 1962 and can be contacted on the Internet at www.scwtca.org. The parent club holds an annual national specialty show, usually in a different city each year, in which many of the country's top SCWTs, handlers and breeders gather to compete. At a specialty show, only members of a single breed are invited to participate. There are also Group specialties, in which all members of a Group are invited. For more information about dog clubs in your area, contact the AKC at www.akc.org on the Internet or write them at their Raleigh, NC address.

HOW SHOWS ARE ORGANIZED
Three kinds of conformation shows are offered by the AKC. There is the all-breed show, in which all AKC-recognized breeds can compete, the specialty show and the Group show.

For a dog to become an AKC champion of record, the dog must earn 15 points at shows. The points must be awarded by at least three different judges and must include two "majors" under different judges. A "major" is a three-, four- or five-point win, and the number of points per win is determined by the number of dogs competing in the show on that day. (Dogs that are absent or are excused are not counted.) The number of points that are awarded varies from breed to breed. More dogs are needed to attain a major in more popular breeds, and fewer dogs are needed in less popular

ON THE MOVE
The truest test of a dog's proper structure is his gait, the way the dog moves. The American Kennel Club defines gait as "the pattern of footsteps at various rates of speed, each pattern distinguished by a particular rhythm and footfall." That the dog moves smoothly and effortlessly indicates to the judge that the dog's structure is well made. From the four-beat gallop, the fastest of canine gaits, to the high-lifting hackney gait, each breed varies in its correct gait; not every breed is expected to move in the same way. Each breed standard defines the correct gait for its breed and often identifies movement faults, such as toeing in, side-winding, over-reaching or crossing over.

Dog shows are enjoyable social events, whether you're competing in the ring or cheering on your fellow fanciers.

breeds. Yearly, the AKC evaluates the number of dogs in competition in each division (there are 14 divisions in all, based on geography) and may or may not change the numbers of dogs required for each number of points. For example, a major in Division 2 (Delaware, New Jersey and Pennsylvania) recently required 17 dogs or 16 bitches for a three-point major, 29 dogs or 27 bitches for a four-point major and 51 dogs or 46 bitches for a five-point major. The SCWT attracts numerically proportionate representation at all-breed shows.

Only one dog and one bitch of each breed can win points at a given show. There are no "co-ed" classes except for champions of record. Dogs and bitches do not compete against each other until they are champions. Dogs that are not champions (referred to as "class dogs") compete in one of

five classes. The class in which a dog is entered depends on age and previous show wins. First there is the Puppy Class (sometimes divided further into classes for 6- to 9-month-olds and 9- to 12-month-olds); next is the Novice Class (for dogs that have no points toward their championship and whose only first-place wins have come in the Puppy Class or the Novice Class, the latter class limited to three first places); then there is the American-bred Class (for dogs bred in the US); the Bred-by-Exhibitor Class (for dogs handled by their breeders or by immediate family members of their breeders) and the Open Class (for any non-champions). Any dog may enter the Open class, regardless of age or win history, but to be competitive the dog should be older and have ring experience.

The judge at the show begins judging the male dogs in the Puppy Class(es) and proceeds through the other classes. The judge awards first through fourth place in each class. The first-place winners of each class then compete with one another in the Winners Class to determine Winners Dog. The judge then starts over with the bitches, beginning with the Puppy Class(es) and proceeding up to the Winners Class to award Winners Bitch, just as he did with the dogs. A Reserve Winners Dog and Reserve Winners Bitch are also selected; they could be awarded the points in the case of a disqualification.

The Winners Dog and Winners Bitch are the two that are awarded the points for their breed. They then go on to compete with any champions of record (often called "specials") of their breed that are entered in the show. The champions may be dogs or bitches; in this class, all are shown together. The judge reviews the Winners Dog and Winners Bitch along with all of the champions to select the Best of Breed winner. The Best of Winners is selected between the Winners Dog and Winners Bitch; if one of these two is selected Best of Breed as well, he or she is automatically determined Best of

Winners. Lastly, the judge selects Best of Opposite Sex to the Best of Breed winner. The Best of Breed winner then goes on to the Group competition.

At a Group or all-breed show, the Best of Breed winners from each breed are divided into their respective groups to compete against one another for Group One through Group Four. Group One (first place) is awarded to the dog that best lives up to the ideal for his breed as described in the standard. A Group judge, therefore, must have a thorough working knowledge of many breed standards. After placements have been made in each Group, the seven Group One winners (from the Sporting Group, Toy Group, Hound Group, etc.) compete against each other for the top honor, Best in Show.

There are different ways to find out about dog shows in your area. The American Kennel Club's monthly magazine, the *American*

Show Wheatens are among the most tolerant souls in the dog world. Being groomed and sculpted is hard work.

Kennel Gazette, is accompanied by the *Events Calendar*; this magazine is available through subscription. You can also look on the AKC's and your parent club's websites for information and check the event listings in your local newspaper.

Your SCWT must be six months of age or older and registered with the AKC in order to be entered in AKC-sanctioned shows in which there are classes for the SCWT. Your SCWT also must not possess any disqualifying faults and must be sexually intact. The reason for the latter is simple: dog shows are the proving grounds to determine which dogs and bitches are worthy of being bred. If they cannot be bred, that defeats the purpose! On that note, only dogs that have achieved championships, thus proving their excellent quality, should be bred. If you have spayed or neutered your dog, however, there are many AKC events other than conforma-tion, such as obedience trials, agility trials and the Canine Good Citizen program, in which you and your SCWT can participate.

OTHER TYPES OF COMPETITION

In addition to conformation shows, the AKC holds a variety of other competitive events. Obedience trials, agility trials and tracking trials are open to all breeds, while hunting tests, field

trials, lure coursing, herding tests and trials, earthdog tests and coonhound events are limited to specific breeds or groups of breeds. The Junior Showmanship program is offered to aspiring young handlers and their dogs, and the Canine Good Citizen® program is an all-around good-behavior test open to all dogs, pure-bred and mixed.

OBEDIENCE TRIALS

Mrs. Helen Whitehouse Walker, a Standard Poodle fancier, can be credited with introducing obedience trials to the United States. In the 1930s she designed a series of exercises based on those of the Associated Sheep, Police, Army Dog Society of Great Britain. These exercises were intended to evaluate the working relationship between dog and owner. Since those early days of the sport in the US, obedience trials have grown more and more popular, and now more than 2,000 trials each year attract over 100,000 dogs and their owners. Any dog registered with the AKC, regardless of neutering or other disqualifications that would preclude entry in conformation competition, can participate in obedience trials.

There are three levels of difficulty in obedience competi-tion. The first (and easiest) level is the Novice, in which dogs can earn the Companion Dog (CD) title. The intermediate level is the Open level, in which the Companion Dog Excellent (CDX) title is awarded. The advanced level is the Utility level, in which dogs compete for the Utility Dog (UD) title. Classes at each level are further divided into "A" and "B," with "A" for beginners and "B" for those with more experience. In order to win a title at a given level, a dog must earn three "legs." A "leg" is accomplished when a dog scores 170 or higher (200 is a perfect score). The scoring system gets a little trickier when you understand that a dog must score more than 50% of the points available for each exercise in order to actually earn the points. Available points for each exercise range between 20 and 40.

A dog must complete different exercises at each level of obedience. The Novice exercises are the easiest, with the Open and finally the Utility levels progressing in difficulty. Examples of Novice exercises are on- and off-lead heeling, a figure-8 pattern, performing a recall (or come), long sit and long down and standing for examination. In the Open level, the Novice-level exercises are required again, but this time without a leash and for longer durations. In addition, the dog must clear a broad jump, retrieve over a jump and drop on recall. In the Utility level, the exercises are quite difficult, including executing basic commands based on hand signals, following a complex heeling pattern, locating articles based on scent discrimination and completing jumps at the handler's direction.

Once he's earned the UD title, a dog can go on to win the prestigious title of Utility Dog Excellent (UDX) by winning "legs" in ten shows. Additionally, Utility Dogs who win "legs" in Open B and Utility B earn points toward the lofty title of Obedience Trial Champion (OTCh.). Established in 1977 by the AKC, this title requires a dog to earn 100 points as well as three first places in a combination of Open B and Utility B classes under three different judges. The "brass ring" of obedience competition is the AKC's National Obedience Invitational. The title at stake here is that of National Obedience Champion (NOC).

Wheatens aren't just beautiful, they're smart and trainable too! This SCWT is performing in an obedience show, easily clearing a jump.

CANINE GOOD CITIZEN® PROGRAM

Have you ever considered getting your dog "certified"? The AKC's Canine Good Citizen® Program affords your dog just that opportunity. Your dog shows that he is a well-behaved canine citizen, using the basic training and good manners you have taught him, by taking a series of ten tests that illustrate that he can behave properly at home, in a public place and around other dogs. The tests are administered by participating dog clubs, colleges, 4-H clubs, Scouts and other community groups and are open to all pure-bred and mixed-breed dogs. Upon passing the ten tests, the suffix CGC is then applied to your dog's name.

AGILITY TRIALS

Agility trials became sanctioned by the AKC in August 1994, when the first licensed agility trials were held. Since that time, agility certainly has grown in popularity by leaps and bounds, literally! The AKC allows all registered breeds (including Miscellaneous Class breeds) to participate, providing the dog is 12 months of age or older. Agility is designed so that the handler demonstrates how well the dog can work at his side. The handler directs his dog through, over, under and around an obstacle course that includes jumps, tires, the dog walk, weave poles, pipe tunnels, collapsed tunnels and more. While working

his way through the course, the dog must keep one eye and ear on the handler and the rest of his body on the course. The handler runs along with the dog, giving verbal and hand signals to guide the dog through the course.

Agility trials are a great way to keep your dog active, and they will keep you running, too! You should join a local agility club to learn more about the sport. These clubs offer sessions in which you can introduce your dog to the various obstacles as well as training classes to prepare him for competition. In no time, your dog will be climbing A-frames, crossing the dog walk and flying over hurdles, all with you right beside him. Your heart will leap every time your dog jumps through the hoop—and you'll be having just as much (if not more) fun!

TRACKING

Tracking tests are exciting ways to test your SCWT's instinctive scenting ability on a competitive level. All dogs have a nose, and all breeds are welcome in tracking tests. The first AKC-licensed tracking test took place in 1937 as part of the Utility level at an obedience trial, and thus competitive tracking was officially begun. The first title, Tracking Dog (TD), was offered in 1947, ten years after the first official tracking test. It was not until 1980 that the AKC added the title

Tracking Dog Excellent (TDX), which was followed by the title Versatile Surface Tracking (VST) in 1995. Champion Tracker (CT) is awarded to a dog who has earned all three of those titles.

The TD level is the first and most basic level in tracking, progressing in difficulty to the TDX and then the VST. A dog must follow a track laid by a human 30 to 120 minutes prior in order to earn the TD title. The track is about 500 yards long and contains up to 5 directional changes. At the next level, the TDX, the dog must follow a 3- to 5-hour-old track over a course that is up to 1,000 yards long and has up to 7 directional changes. In the most difficult level, the VST, the track is up to 5 hours old and located in an urban setting.

OTHER ACTIVITIES FOR WHEATENS

Given the many activities that the AKC sponsors, the SCWT is limited in which areas it can compete. As a long-legged terrier, the breed is not permitted to compete in Earthdog events. The breed is not a digging terrier like the Scottie or the Norwich Terrier, so Wheaten owners do not feel unjustly excluded.

Despite the breed's considerable talent as a herding dog, the SCWT is not permitted to compete in AKC-sponsored herding tests and trials. This has not daunted

the spirit of some Wheaten owners. Near Sacramento each year, there is a herding clinic and instinct test, organized by the SCWT Club of Northern California, and there is usually a very high pass rate. Other SCWTs are Herding Capability Tested (HCT) with the American Herding Breeds Association, an organization that encourages owners to nurture their dogs' natural abilities as herders. Many Wheatens of yesteryear worked as farm dogs and their herding ability is rightly impressive.

Another area that SCWTs excel is flyball, in which the breed has reached high acclaim. Some Wheatens have earned the title of Flyball Masters. Sometimes, however, SCWTs compete in non-sanctioned fun matches and events sponsored by organizations outside the jurisdiction of the AKC.

Agile and enthusiastic, the SCWT takes to obedience and agility trials with ease. These competitive events are great exercise and fun for dog and owner alike.

INDEX

My Soft Coated Wheaten Terrier

PUT YOUR PUPPY'S FIRST PICTURE HERE

Dog's Name _____

Date _____ Photographer _____